Disclaimer

Every effort has been made to ensure that the information contained within this guide is accurate at the time of publication. How2become Ltd is not responsible for anyone failing any part of any selection process as a result of the information contained within this guide. How2become Ltd and their authors cannot accept any responsibility for any errors or omissions within this guide, however caused. No responsibility for loss or damage occasioned by any person acting, or refraining from action, as a result of the material in this publication can be accepted by How2become Ltd.

The information within this guide does not represent the views of any third party service or organisation.

how2become

The Bar Course Aptitude Test Guide (BCAT)

www.How2Become.com

As part of this product you have also received FREE access to online tests that will help you to pass the BCAT.

To gain access, simply go to:

www.PsychometricTestsOnline.co.uk

Get more products for passing any test or interview at:

www.how2become.com

CONTENTS

INTRODUCTION

About the BCAT

Those seeking a job in the legal profession have to undergo a strict and difficult selection process. The Bar Course Aptitude Test (BCAT) is the first step of a candidate's training process for becoming a barrister and it is this step which marks the beginning of a long journey into a challenging but rewarding career.

This book will cover everything you will need to know about the BCAT and the process involved. This book has been created to ensure a candidate is fully prepared for their test, and is given all the information required to pass their BCAT. Whilst a person cannot truly study for the test, they can help themselves by taking lots of practice tests and become familiar with the testing process.

By the end of this book, you will be able to:

- Show an ability to differentiate between inferences, abstractions and generalisations through applying logical and critical interpretation.
- Demonstrate high levels of critical thinking and logical understanding.
- Recognise strong and weak arguments.
- Evaluate arguments and their accuracy.
- Focus on important evidence to generate sufficient support and justification.
- Separate facts from opinion and assumption.

WHAT IS THE BCAT?

The BCAT is a form of psychometric testing which assesses a person's level of performance. The test is designed for anyone wishing to pursue a career in the legal sector, specifically for aspiring barristers. Since 2013, the test has been made compulsory, thus, anyone wishing to undertake a Bar Professional Training course (BPTC), needs to pass the Bar Course Aptitude Test (BCAT) prior to applying for the BPTC. The test is created to ensure that only the candidates with the potential to pass the BPTC undertake the test.

Although passing this test does not necessarily guarantee that you will be a good barrister, it can however give some indication as to whether or not you may be cut out for the position.

Based on the Watson-Glaser critical thinking appraisal, the Bar Course Aptitude Test (BCAT) is a useful tool to measure a candidate's abilities and skills required to become a barrister.

It is a test that aims to explore a person's intellectual and cognitive skills, both in terms of logic and critical understanding. The test assesses all the core skills that are essential requirements for the BPTC; all of which are mandatory in the life of a barrister. Barristers need to be able to demonstrate high levels of critical understanding to ensure thorough and accurate results.

HOW IS THE BCAT MEASURED?

Foremost, the BCAT is used to measure a candidate's critical thinking and reasoning skills to demonstrate their suitability and competency for the job role.

Becoming a barrister is a challenging process. These tests are specifically designed to test candidate's abilities and critical thinking skills in order to make sure they are up for the job. The job role requires you to think on your feet, think outside the box and take every possibility into consideration. Thus this test will primarily deal with assessing a candidate's suitability and measure their competencies and skills required.

Critical thinking can be defined as 'thinking logically - using an objective approach to evaluate arguments and using relevant information to draw conclusions'. To be presented with a particular situation and being able to engage in different understandings and perspectives is an important role of barristers.

The term 'critical thinking' can be structured through an organised framework which helps to facilitate high levels of knowledge and awareness. The **"RED Model"** is a way of breaking down the most important and valuable elements of the critical thinking process; in order to provide an in-depth account of a situation with truth, accuracy and integrity.

THE "RED MODEL"

Here is a table displaying the **"RED Model"** and the important skills required for any aspiring barrister:

Recognising Assumptions	Evaluate Arguments	Draw Conclusions
• Identifying assumptions is an important element for any aspiring barrister.	• **Evaluating** arguments entails objective and accurate **analysis**.	• Piecing together all the information, **evidence** and facts to arrive at a **conclusion** is the most important part of the process.
• It is deceptive to assume that the information you are given to be complete fact.	• Being able to identify weak **arguments** and gaps in missing **evidence** is crucial.	• The **logic** of the decision must be accountable through **evidence** and **justification**.
• You need to consider every inch of the **evidence** and justify its logic and validity.	• Questioning the strength of an argument and understanding mitigating circumstances is a vital skill to the role.	• Candidates who are able to show no generalisations in the process and are able to change their view if required, are candidates who are described as having **"good judgement"**.
• Identifying and questioning the difference between **truth** and **assumption** is imperative.	• The job requires a person to remain **objective**. They cannot be seen to get emotionally attached or share their viewpoints.	
• Such unfound **logic** and uncertainty helps reveal missing aspects of the truth.	• They act as an **impartial** judge who subsequently tries to gather up as much information as possible.	• The art of any candidate being able to show levels of **integrity**, will power and **determination** will help to find the best possible conclusion.
• Looking at things from different angles is a useful way to **analyse** indefinite circumstances.		

The "Red Model" can be used as a guideline in order for you to complete the BCAT. These are typical steps that you could follow when assessing arguments, conclusions and assumptions.

The BCAT requires you to think logically. In order for you to do this, you have to think carefully about everything you read and everything you are told. You need to be able to recognise if the proposed argument or conclusion is accurate and justified. Can the conclusion or assumption be reached by what you have been told? Is there any significant information missing which is needed in order to make that final conclusion?

Remember, this test is based on facts. You cannot answer these questions based on personal views or what you know to be true. You have to take each question at face value, and remember, you can only come to the conclusion based on what you've read, not what you think!

WHAT TO EXPECT

The BCAT format uses statements and conclusions; of which the candidate must answer in a particular way depending on the type of question they are answering. The test consists of 5 basic question types, all of which will appear on your real BCAT. Each question type is used in order to assess a particular skill or ability that is required and used in the role of a barrister. The five question types are as follows:

Inference	A conclusion that can be drawn from facts or supposed facts.
Recognition of Assumptions	Something that is presupposed or anticipated. Something that is often taken for granted.
Deduction	The ability to come to a conclusion based on the information you are provided with.
Interpretation	How you interpret and understand the statement, in order to form a conclusion.
Evaluation of Arguments	Measuring an argument's strengths and weaknesses to determine how well it forms a solid argument.

In the real BCAT, you will be provided with these 5 testing sections. For each question, you will decide what answer appears most appropriate. Your score will depend on the number of questions you answer correctly, and so you should try to answer all the questions, even if you are not sure on the correct answer.

The BCAT has a time limit. The time limit is 55 minutes, of which there are 60 questions in total. You need to make sure that you work quickly and efficiently through the questions, without sacrificing accuracy.

HOW AM I SCORED?

At the end of your BCAT, you will receive your score. Candidates will receive a computer generated feedback sheet on the day of their test. On the feedback sheet, candidates will either receive a 'pass', a 'marginal fail' or a 'significant fail'.

A 'pass' mark means that you are now able to enrol onto the Bar Professional Training Course (BPTC). However, people who score a 'significant fail' may want to reconsider their next step. This test is a mere indication of the level of difficulty to expect from the BPTC; however this course will be notably more difficult than the BCAT. If you fail to pass, you may need to reconsider whether the job of a barrister is right for you.

Note: please be aware that we cannot give you an exact number of how many marks you will need to pass the BCAT. The number of exact marks is not available, but is claimed by the Bar Standards Board that the grade boundary to pass is set quite low; and the majority of candidates do pass. The pass mark is set quite low in order to filter strong candidates from the weak.

HOW TO WORK THROUGH THE BOOK

Although you are given only 60 questions in the real BCAT, this book purposely provides you with lots of sample questions in order for you to gain a clear understanding of what to expect and to help you fully prepare for your real test.

The book covers all the essential information you will need to know about the BCAT. From tips for passing the BCAT, to details of the test itself and of course, lots of sample of questions for you to work through, this guide will undoubtedly improve your BCAT performance.

The book follows a simple structure that will allow you to get to grips with each testing question. You will be able to work through lots of sample questions in each chapter at your own pace and then check your answers with the detailed explanations we have provided you with. Be sure to check all of your answers! It is just as important to know where you went wrong as getting the questions right. You need to understand why the right answer is correct and understand where you went wrong in your thought process to learn from for future reference.

The book will be broken down into eight chapters. The first five chapters will refer to one of five question types that will be assessed on the test. So, **inference, recognition of assumptions, deduction, interpretation and evaluation of arguments** will form the headings for each chapter. For each of these chapters, you will be given a description of what the question type means, how you will be scored and sample questions for you to answer. You will then be able to check your answers.

Chapter 6 is the mock test chapter. You will be given the opportunity to undergo a practice test for the Bar Course Aptitude Test. Like the real test, you will be given 60 questions which you should try to answer in the time limit. The time limit for the test is 55 minutes. You need to try and answer the questions as quickly as possible without sacrificing accuracy. This will give you some understanding of your critical thinking abilities and your chances of success at becoming a barrister.

After completing your mock test in chapter 6, you will then be able to use chapter 7 to evaluate your scores. Chapter 7 includes a detailed scoring criteria that you can refer to throughout the test if you wish. The criteria gives you key information, which you should remember when answering any of the questions.

The final chapter, chapter 8, is a basic FAQ's and information chapter. You may have lots of questions prior to taking the BCAT and we have provided you with the important information you might want to know.

Remember: stay focused, stay critical and carefully consider each statement before answering the question.

Finally, we have also provided you with some additional free online psychometric tests which will help to further improve your competence in this particular testing area. To gain access, simply go to:

www.PsychometricTestsOnline.co.uk

Good luck and best wishes,

The how2become team

The How2become team

TIPS FOR PASSING THE BAR COURSE APTITUDE TEST (BCAT)

In order for you to be fully prepared for the BCAT, you need to be able to demonstrate high levels of critical thinking and other core skills. To help you pass your test, we have provided you with a list of tips that may help you focus on everything you will need to know to pass the Bar Course Aptitude Test:

- **You need to ask yourself basic questions.** 'What is going on?', 'What do I know from this?', 'What doesn't this tell me?', 'What is being taken for granted?'. Such questions will allow you to probe deeper into the information you are provided with and spot errors or assumptions in the information provided.

- **Rate the quality of information.** You need to be able to demonstrate your ability to identify underlying assumptions and the impact this causes on the validity of the information. Rate each assumption by asking questions such as 'how likely is this assumption to be true?', 'how can we assume this to be true?', 'are there any other possible assumptions to take into consideration?'

- **Question your assumptions.** Do they make sense? Look at things from all angles. Don't just rely on your initial assumption. Try and look at other alternatives.

- **Read carefully.** A common mistake amongst these tests is that candidates do not read the question or statement properly. Be sure to take your time reading everything carefully to ensure you answer the question correctly.

- **The "RED Model".** The "Red Model" refers to recognising, evaluating and drawing conclusions. Make sure you follow each step. This model will allow you to conduct clear and concise reasoning and demonstrate your critical approach.

- **An objective and balanced approach.** Be sure to look for clear, precise and relevant information. You need to be able to distinguish between what is fact and what can be assumed. You need to find evidence to support your claim. You need to be able to remain objective. Take a step back and look at a situation from a retrospective point of view.

- **Evaluate.** Try to identify multiple possibilities based on the evidence and facts you are presented with. Make sure you explore all the important information you are provided with and evaluate its strength in terms of argument validity and accuracy.

CHAPTER 1

Inferences

In the BCAT, you will be required to answer questions based on the five abilities, as mentioned in the Introduction. In Chapter 1, you will focus on questions regarding **Inferences**. The term inference can be used to describe conclusions that can be drawn from supposed facts and observations. Although inferences are based on possible facts, it does by no means provide a correct nor accurate account of the truth; it is a mere depiction of a 'possibility' that may or may not be the truth.

Inferences are an intellectual act by which one can conclude something is true on the basis of something else being true, or seeming to be true. Inferences can be accurate or inaccurate, logical or illogical, justified or unjustified. You simply need to take these inferences at face value and accept what the statement is telling you.

For example, if you pass a house which has its lights on, you could infer that someone is home. However this may not be true. Although the lights may be on, the house may be completely empty. The occupants of the house may have their lights on because they forgot to turn them off. Or maybe they left them on to make it look like someone was in. By all accounts, any of these scenarios could be possibilities and all these scenarios can therefore be referred to as inferences.

In this chapter, you will be provided with 30 sample questions. You will be given a statement which you are to regard as true. For each statement, you will then be given a possible inference which could be drawn from the statement. You will have to work through each question and determine the degree of falseness or accuracy.

Please note that we have purposely provided you with no time limit. This is so you can work through these questions slowly and carefully, to ensure you understand what is expected, and how to answer the questions correctly.

HOW TO ANSWER THE QUESTION

For each inference, you will be given a choice of 5 possible answers: **True, Probably True, Insufficient Data, Probably False** and **False**.

You must tick the box which seems most accurate and reasonable.

ANSWER OPTIONS

Tick **True** if you believe the inference follows reasonable logic to the statement provided.

Tick **Probably True** if you think it is more than likely to be true than false, but holds no solid evidence.

Tick **Insufficient Data** if you think that you are unable to tell from the statement provided. You have nothing to base your judgements on.

Tick **Probably False** if you think that it is more likely to be false than true.

Tick **False** if you believe that it is wrong because it either misinterprets the facts given or contradicts the statement in some way.

EXAMPLE 1

Statement:

One hundred and fifty students from a secondary school voluntarily attended a protest to show their views on animal testing. At the protest, the main view displayed was that animal testing was "inhumane, unfair and morally wrong". This topic was selected as one of the most problematic amongst the Environmental Science students. They showed a strong belief against animal testing and displayed a sense of moral obligation to defend animals from animal cruelty.

Proposed Inference:

As a group of students, they showed passion about environmental problems more so than other students at their school.

True	Probably True	Insufficient Data	Probably False	False
	✓			

Answer Example 1 - Feedback:

In example 1, the proposed inference is Probably True. Generally, most students do not show serious concerns in regards to animal testing. It is not a topic that is often considered amongst young adults. It cannot be considered definitely true because the facts in the statement do not indicate how much interest other students may or may not have, so you would be relying on a heavy assumption. It is also possible that some of the students who went on protest only went because other people were and not because they have a real sense of moral obligation to express their views, suggesting it cannot be 100% true.

EXAMPLE 2

Statement:

One hundred and fifty students from a secondary school voluntarily attended a protest to show their views on animal testing. At the protest, the main view displayed was that animal testing was "inhumane, unfair and morally wrong". This topic was selected as one of the most problematic amongst the Environmental Science students. They showed a strong belief against animal testing and displayed a sense of moral obligation to defend animals from animal cruelty.

Proposed Inference:

The Environmental Science students were currently studying animal testing.

True	Probably True	Insufficient Data	Probably False	False
		✓		

Answer Example 2 - Feedback:

In example 2, the proposed inference shows Insufficient Data for making a judgement. The statement does not indicate that the students are currently studying animal testing. They may have studied it a while ago. They may not have studied it at all. Therefore you cannot make this inference.

Now it's your turn!

INFERENCE TESTING QUESTIONS

QUESTION 1

Statement:

Women's organisations in India have welcomed the amendment of the Industrial Employment Rules 1946 to control sexual harassments in the work place.

Proposed Inference:

Sexual harassment in India has become more problematic compared to other developed countries.

True	Probably True	Insufficient Data	Probably False	False
		X		

QUESTION 2

Statement:

Women's organisations in India have welcomed the amendment of the Industrial Employment Rules 1946 to control sexual harassments in the work place.

Proposed Inference:

Many organisations in India will stop recruiting women in order to avoid sexual harassment issues.

True	Probably True	Insufficient Data	Probably False	False
		X		

QUESTION 3

Statement:

It would be in everyone's interest to make CV's anonymous to give everyone the same equal chance. It is argued that name, gender, photographs, race etc should all be removed so candidates are selected based on performance, skill and experience.

Proposed Inference:

The argument is based on minimising discrimination based on gender, race and appearance.

True	Probably True	Insufficient Data	Probably False	False
X				

QUESTION 4

Statement:

The case of a Mumbai couple who approached the courts in India after their time limit for an abortion was overdue, wanted a termination of their pregnancy. This case of euthanasia was denied by the courts. The parents wanted to be granted permission for an abortion after they found out that the foetus had been detected to have disabilities which would affect the life of the unborn child. The courts argued that the unborn child has the right to live despite being possibly disabled.

Proposed Inference:

The courts in India have the right and authority to sanction euthanasia.

True	Probably True	Insufficient Data	Probably False	False
	X			

QUESTION 5

Statement:

The case of a Mumbai couple who approached the courts in India after their time limit for an abortion was overdue, wanted a termination of their pregnancy. This case of euthanasia was denied by the courts. The parents wanted to be granted permission for an abortion after they found out that the foetus had been detected to have disabilities which would affect the life of the unborn child. The courts argued that the unborn child has the right to live despite being possibly disabled.

Proposed Inference:

The courts consider how far along a woman is in her pregnancy before granting permission for an abortion.

True	Probably True	Insufficient Data	Probably False	False
X				

QUESTION 6

Statement:

The case of a Mumbai couple who approached the courts in India after their time limit for an abortion was overdue, wanted a termination of their pregnancy. This case of euthanasia was denied by the courts. The parents wanted to be granted permission for an abortion after they found out that the foetus had been detected to have disabilities which would affect the life of the unborn child. The courts argued that the unborn child has the right to live despite being possibly disabled.

Proposed Inference:

The courts of Mumbai believe that the child has no rights because it is unborn.

True	Probably True	Insufficient Data	Probably False	False
				X

QUESTION 7

Statement:

A local shopkeeper was giving a statement to the police. He told them; as he closed up his shop for the night and switched off the lights, a person appeared wearing a balaclava and a hoody and demanded money from the till. The shopkeeper opened the cashier and the money was scooped up. The person scarpered from the shop and the police were called shortly after.

Proposed Inference:

The robber was a man.

True	Probably True	Insufficient Data	Probably False	False
		X		

QUESTION 8

Statement:

A local shopkeeper was giving a statement to the police. He told them; as he closed up his shop for the night and switched off the lights, a person appeared wearing a balaclava and a hoody and demanded money from the till. The shopkeeper opened the cashier and the money was taken. The person scarpered from the shop and the police were called shortly after.

Proposed Inference:

The shopkeeper scooped up the money and handed it over to the robber.

True	Probably True	Insufficient Data	Probably False	False
	X	X		

QUESTION 9

Statement:

A murder investigation was taking place. There were 6 suspects in which the police had, all of which were related to gang culture. The victim was also believed to be part of a gang, but 'wanted out'. All of the suspects were known to be near the scene of the crime when the murder took place. They all had motives for killing the victim. One suspect has been declared not guilty.

Proposed Inference:

The murder was related to gang culture.

True	Probably True	Insufficient Data	Probably False	False
	X			

QUESTION 10

Statement:

Studies have indicated that people who live in the North of England are far more likely to suffer with heart disease as opposed to people living in the South. There is a clear distinction between the northerners and southerners which can be related to salary. The average income for southerners is somewhat higher than the average income for northerners.

Proposed Inference:

People who earn more income have a better lifestyle and therefore are less likely to suffer with heart disease.

True	Probably True	Insufficient Data	Probably False	False
	X			

QUESTION 11

Statement:

Studies have indicated that people who live in the North of England are far more likely to suffer with heart disease as opposed to people living in the South. There is a clear distinction between the northerners and southerners which can be related to salary. The average income for southerners is somewhat higher than the average income for northerners.

Proposed Inference:

Location makes no difference to whether or not people develop heart disease.

True	Probably True	Insufficient Data	Probably False	False
				X

QUESTION 12

Statement:

A teacher was stabbed in a classroom. The police have cornered off the school and are questioning her students. She was stabbed twice, once in the leg and once in the chest. The police have called this act of violence as 'disgusting'. The police are awaiting confirmations on the whereabouts of students and staff.

Proposed inference:

The police are investigating a murder.

True	Probably True	Insufficient Data	Probably False	False
		X		

good point → *unlawful killing of another human being.*

QUESTION 13

Statement:

An MP has suggested lowering the age of consent to 13. However, some people do not agree with this change. They argue that lowering the age of consent to 13 will only put young girls at a more vulnerable position. They say that "13 is too young. They are naïve and immature and have no idea of what they will be getting in to". A woman speaks out who was raped at the age of 15 and claims that these children "will be scarred for life".

Proposed Inference:

Lowering the age of consent to 13 will put children at more risk of sexual abuse.

True	Probably True	Insufficient Data	Probably False	False
✗				

QUESTION 14

Statement:

An MP has debated lowering the age of consent to 13. However, some people do not agree with this change. They argue that lowering the age of consent to 13 will only put young girls at a more vulnerable position. They say that "13 is too young. They are naïve and immature and have no idea of what they will be getting in to". A woman speaks out who was raped at the age of 15 and claims that these children "will be scarred for life".

Proposed Inference:

More teenagers under the current age of consent are having sex.

True	Probably True	Insufficient Data	Probably False	False
		✗		

QUESTION 15

Statement:

The Chinese Government implemented a policy in the late 1970's to address and reduce the country's birth rate. They decided to introduce a one-child policy to create benefits such as access to education and better healthcare. However, in recent years, this policy has become somewhat relaxed. Chinese citizens are now able to apply to have a second child if their first child is a girl, or if both parents were only-children. In 2008, China's population slowly increased to 1.3 billion.

Proposed Inference:

Women who become pregnant after their first child are forced to have an abortion and forced to be sterilized.

True	Probably True	Insufficient Data	Probably False	False
			✗	

QUESTION 16

Statement:

The Chinese Government implemented a policy in the late 1970's to address and reduce the country's birth rate. They decided to introduce a one-child policy to create benefits such as access to education and better healthcare. However, in recent years, this policy has become somewhat relaxed. Chinese citizens are now able to apply to have a second child if their first child is a girl, or if both parents were only-children. In 2008, China's population slowly increased to 1.3 billion.

Proposed Inference:

The one-child policy was implemented by the Chinese Government to tackle the rising population of the country.

True	Probably True	Insufficient Data	Probably False	False
	✗			

QUESTION 17

Statement:

The Chinese Government implemented a policy in the late 1970's to address and reduce the country's birth rate. They decided to introduce a one-child policy to create benefits such as access to education and better healthcare. However, in recent years, this policy has become somewhat relaxed. Chinese citizens are now able to apply to have a second child if their first child is a girl, or if both parents were only-children. In 2008, China's population slowly increased to 1.3 billion.

Proposed Inference:

Previous Chinese Governments had discouraged people to have large families.

True	Probably True	Insufficient Data	Probably False	False
			X	

QUESTION 18

Statement:

In the personnel department, there are a lot of employees who work there as a technician. Most of these technicians provide specialist knowledge and understanding for test developments. Rebecca Walker works in the personnel department.

Proposed Inference:

Rebecca Walker is a technician in the personnel department.

True	Probably True	Insufficient Data	Probably False	False
	X	X		

QUESTION 19

Statement:

In 2000, the Race Relations Act was introduced. It aims to reduce racial discrimination and promote equality and opportunity amongst different races. The act was implemented so that all schools, colleges and universities were obligated to follow it to demonstrate their values of equal opportunities. The Act plays a vital role in the planning, policy making, learning and teaching quality in the public service sector.

Proposed Inference:

The Race Relations Act of 2000 will stop racial discrimination completely.

True	Probably True	Insufficient Data	Probably False	False
			X	

QUESTION 20

Statement:

In 2000, the Race Relations Act was introduced. It aims to reduce racial discrimination and promote equality and opportunity amongst different races. The act was implemented so that all schools, colleges and universities were obligated to follow it demonstrate their values of equal opportunity. The Act plays a vital role in the planning, policy making, learning and teaching quality in the public service sector.

Proposed Inference:

The Race Relations Act 2000 puts the minority at a disadvantage.

True	Probably True	Insufficient Data	Probably False	False
				X

QUESTION 21

Statement:

Technological change has a huge impact on industries. These changes also affect software developments and service industries. Airlines, insurance companies and managerial positions often rely on new advances of technology. Over the years, it has become apparent that the future of technological changes are inevitable.

Proposed Inference:

Technological change will affect specific functions of an organisation, leaving other areas of the organisation undisturbed.

True	Probably True	Insufficient Data	Probably False	False
			X	

QUESTION 22

Statement:

Technological change has a huge impact on industries. These changes also affect software developments and service industries. Airlines, insurance companies and managerial positions often rely on new advances of technology. Over the years, it has become apparent that the future of technological changes are inevitable.

Proposed Inference:

Technological change has already started.

True	Probably True	Insufficient Data	Probably False	False
X				

QUESTION 23

Statement:

Sixty students attended an art exhibition. The exhibition was split into four different sections: the works of Andy Warhol, sculptures, 3D Art and paintings. These four topics were all relevant for the students as it will inspire their next art project.

Proposed Inference:

Most of these students had not discussed these topics in their schools prior to the exhibition.

True	Probably True	Insufficient Data	Probably False	False
		X	X	

QUESTION 24

Statement:

A group of friends walk through the subway after a night out. They come across a man who is lying on the floor on some cardboard with a blanket thrown over him. His appearance is all scruffy and dirty and is holding on to his pet dog, shivering. He has a bin bag with what appears to contain some clothes and tins of food.

Proposed Inference:

The man is homeless.

True	Probably True	Insufficient Data	Probably False	False
	X			

QUESTION 25

Statement:

A group of friends walk through the subway after a night out. They come across a man who is lying on the floor on some cardboard with a blanket thrown over him. His appearance is all scruffy and dirty and is holding on to his pet dog, shivering. He has a bin bag with what appears to contain some clothes and tins of food.

Proposed Inference:

The group of friends stopped to ask the man if he was ok.

True	Probably True	Insufficient Data	Probably False	False
		X		

QUESTION 26

Statement:

In India, breast cancer has been on the increase, with an estimated 80,000 new cases diagnosed each year. Breast cancer increased approximately 50% between 1965 and 1985. This increase is said to be associated with an improved life expectancy and greater urbanisation.

Proposed Inference:

People who are living longer are less likely to get breast cancer.

True	Probably True	Insufficient Data	Probably False	False
			X	X

QUESTION 27

Statement:

In India, breast cancer has been on the increase, with an estimated 80,000 new cases diagnosed each year. Breast cancer increased approximately 50% between 1965 and 1985. This increase is said to be associated with an improved lifestyles, longer life expectancies and greater urbanisation.

Proposed Inference:

India's breast cancer rate is much higher than other countries.

True	Probably True	Insufficient Data	Probably False	False
		X		

QUESTION 28

Statement:

Child labour has always been a significant global issue associated with poverty, inadequate education, lack of opportunity and a range of health issues. Developing countries such as Africa, Asia and Latin America are among the biggest countries in which child labour is at its highest. Such working conditions jeopardise children's health and lifestyles. They are made to work at a very young age, are malnourished and work long hours in unpleasant working conditions.

Proposed Inference:

Less developed countries use child labour as a way of maintaining workforces.

True	Probably True	Insufficient Data	Probably False	False

QUESTION 29

Statement:

Child labour has always been a significant global issue associated with poverty, inadequate education, lack of opportunity and a range of health issues. Developing countries such as Africa, Asia and Latin America are among the biggest countries in which child labour is at its highest. Such working conditions jeopardise children's health and lifestyles. They are made to work at a very young age, are malnourished and work long hours in unpleasant working conditions.

Proposed Inference:

Child labour is only occurring in developing countries and not countries that are already developed.

True	Probably True	Insufficient Data	Probably False	False

QUESTION 30

Statement:

The role of the equal opportunities policy has been implemented in the UK. This policy is in aid to tackle the issues of inequality in the workplace. Providing equal opportunities in the workplace will reduce discrimination and provide a sense of equality amongst race, culture, religion, sex, age or disability. The monitoring of the equal opportunities policy will ensure the recruitment process or workforce is not effected by inequality or unfair conditions.

Proposed Inference:

The Government of the UK are concerned with the importance of demonstrating high levels of equal rights to ensure everyone, of any race, age, gender etc benefits from the policy.

True	Probably True	Insufficient Data	Probably False	False
X				

INFERENCE TEST SECTION – ANSWERS

Q1.

Insufficient Data. There is no evidence to suggest whether this is true or false. You cannot tell from the facts given. One can assume that there are more sexual harassment problems in India compared to other developed countries, but we have no data to suggest how much harassment goes on in India, and how this differs from other developed countries.

Q2.

Probably false. This is unlikely to be the case. It is doubtful that organisations will stop recruiting women to prevent sexual harassment from occurring.

Q3.

True. The aim of this argument is to reduce the risk of discrimination based on race, gender and appearance. This claim is reasonable to make based on the data provided.

Q4.

True. The couple went to the courts because they have the power to sanction euthanasia and therefore the inference must be true.

Q5.

Probably true. The courts are more than likely to take into consideration how far along the woman is in her pregnancy before granting permission for an abortion. However, there is no solid evidence to suggest this, so the claim is most probably true.

Q6.

False. The statement clearly indicates that the courts believe "that the unborn child has rights to live despite being possibly disabled". So therefore, this proposed claim is false.

Q7.

Insufficient data. There is no evidence to suggest that the robber was a man or a woman and therefore this conclusion cannot be drawn.

Q8.

Insufficient data. There is no evidence as to whether it was the shopkeeper or the robber who scooped up the money. Therefore this conclusion cannot be drawn.

Q9.

Probably true. It is more than likely that the murder that took place was related to gang culture. However, there is no solid evidence to suggest it is definitely true. The fact that all the people were related in a gang and the victim was too, suggests it is probably true.

Q10.

Probably true. It is likely that having a bigger income suggests a better lifestyle and therefore is more than likely going to help people avoid heart disease compared to people with lower incomes.

Q11.

False. This inference is wrong due to the statement claiming a difference in relation to lifestyles and incomes. This contradicts the facts being clearly stated.

Q12.

Insufficient data. There is no evidence to suggest whether or not the teacher had been murdered. You cannot tell from the facts provided because it only states that she was stabbed, and not the severity of the case.

Q13.

Probably true. This is more than likely to be true. At the age of 13, children are more likely to feel pressurised and abused in terms of sexual relations. However, there is no clear evidence to suggest that this will be the case.

Q14.

Probably true. This is more than likely to be true. The claims to lower the age of consent is an indication that children are already having sex below the age of consent.

Q15.

Probably false. There is no evidence to back up this claim, but you can assume that this is most probably false.

Q16.

True. This follows a reasonable and accurate account of the facts provided. The facts in the statement clearly indicate that the country faces a population issue which needs to be tackled, so therefore this inference is definitely true.

Q17.

Probably false. If previous governments had discouraged people to have large families, then the population would not have been in crisis and therefore the new government wouldn't have had to implement the one child policy. Therefore, it is more likely to be false than true.

Q18.

Insufficient data. The facts give no indication as to whether Rebecca is a technician just because she works in the Personnel department. You cannot tell from the facts provided and therefore the data provided is not sufficient enough to come to that conclusion.

Q19.

Probably false. There is no way to indicate the future of racial discrimination based on the statement provided. This is more than likely to be false because generally, not everyone will comply with the law enforcement and it is obvious that racial discrimination will continue to exist to some extent.

Q20.

False. The Race Relations 2000 Act was implemented to help the minorities and reduce racial discrimination. Therefore, this statement is false.

Q21.

Insufficient data. There is no evidence or information to suggest that certain areas of an organisation will not be affected from technological change. You cannot tell from these facts provided and therefore there is no sufficient data.

Q22.

Probably true. This inference is more than likely to be true. Despite no evidence to suggest that this is the case, it seems most reasonable. General knowledge indicates that technological change is currently taking place.

Q23.

Probably false. It is more than likely that these students had been learning or briefly spoke about these topics before attending the exhibition, so therefore the inference is probably false.

Q24.

Probably true. It is more than likely that the man is homeless. However, it is not definitely true, because we are not given enough information, and there might be other circumstances to take into consideration. Therefore we can conclude that the information provided is most probably true.

Q25.

Insufficient data. You cannot tell from the facts provided whether or not the group stopped to ask the man if he was ok, therefore there is no sufficient data to conclude this.

Q26.

Probably false. This inference contradicts the facts provided. The statement suggests that breast cancer is on the increase possibly because of 'improved life expectancy'. Therefore people living longer, are said to be more likely at risk.

Q27.

Insufficient data. You cannot tell by the facts provided as to whether India has a higher rate of breast cancer than other countries. No other countries are mentioned and therefore there is no sufficient evidence to suggest this to be true.

Q28.

Probably true. This is more than likely to be true. Less developed countries still rely on child labourers to assist their workforces.

Q29.

Insufficient data. The statement does not give an indication as to whether child labour only occurs in developing countries, however, it can be inferred that this isn't likely to be the case and that child labour still happens in developed countries.

Q30.

True. The facts in the statement clearly indicate that the equal opportunities policy was implemented to "tackle" inequality amongst races, gender, age, sex etc; therefore the inference must be true.

CHAPTER 2

Recognition of Assumptions

In this part of the BCAT, you will need to be able to recognise and interpret **assumptions**. Assumptions rely on the idea that something is presupposed and therefore, taken for granted.

Assumptions are not always correct, or justifiable. They are something that we take at face value. They form part of our belief system. We assume our beliefs to be true and use them to interpret other things accordingly.

You need to be able to distinguish the difference between inferences and assumptions. As discussed earlier in chapter 1, inferences are a way to conclude whether a statement is true based on something else being true. Whereas, assumptions are something that we learn from prior experience or knowledge and therefore believe it to be true, despite it not necessarily being the case.

Here is an example to demonstrate the difference between inferences and assumptions. A situation sees a man homeless and begging for money. The assumption can be made that people living on the streets are in need of some help. The inference comes from the assumption made that this man is in need of some help. Therefore, this demonstrates that an assumption is a generalised statement which offers a presupposed thought, whereas an inference is something that can be argued to be true based on the facts being provided are also true.

Another example of an assumption is if a person were to say "My graduation is in September", you can assume that the person will be eligible to graduate and has passed their university course. This assumption can be made as it follows on from the previous statement.

In this chapter, you will be provided with 30 sample questions. For each statement, a proposed assumption will follow. You will need to work through each assumption and determine whether that assumption can or cannot be presumed.

Please note that we have purposely not provided you with a time limit. You should work through these questions slowly and carefully, to ensure you understand what is expected, and how to answer the questions correctly.

HOW TO ANSWER THE QUESTION

For each proposed assumption, you will be given a choice of 2 possible answers: **Assumption Made** and **Assumption Not Made.**

You must tick the box which seems most accurate and reasonable.

ANSWER OPTIONS

Tick **assumption made** if you believe that an assumption can be made by the facts provided.

Tick **assumption not made** if you think that an assumption cannot be made by the facts provided.

EXAMPLE 1

Statement:

The aim of education is to create an efficient and reliable workforce.

Proposed Assumption:

People who have a good education are more likely to go on to become compliant and capable workers.

Assumption Made	Assumption Not Made
✓	

Answer Example 1 – Feedback:

It can be assumed that people who have a good education are more likely to prove capable workers.

EXAMPLE 2

Statement:

We want to get to our holiday destination in the quickest possible time, so we will go by plane.

Proposed Assumption:

Travelling by plane will be more convenient than travelling by another means of transportation.

Assumption Made	Assumption Not Made
	✓

Answer Example 2 – Feedback:

This assumption is not made from the statement provided. The statement talks about time saving and not convenience. So therefore, this assumption cannot be made.

RECOGNITION OF ASSUMPTIONS TESTING QUESTIONS

QUESTION 1

Statement:

We want to get to our holiday destination in the quickest possible time, so we will go by plane.

Proposed Assumption:

There is a flight service available to get to their destination.

Assumption Made	Assumption Not Made
✓	

QUESTION 2

Statement:

We want to get to our holiday destination in the quickest possible time, so we will go by plane.

Proposed Assumption:

Going by plane is the fastest way to travel.

Assumption Made	Assumption Not Made
✓	

QUESTION 3

Statement:

The aim of education is to create an efficient and capable workforce.

Proposed Assumption:

Education is the only way which ensures society of compliant workers.

Assumption Made	Assumption Not Made
	✓

QUESTION 4

Statement:

The students from Chile demanded that university education should be free. In 2012, they formed a protest around this topic.

Proposed Assumption:

Students from Chile are unable to afford to go to university and receive a higher education.

Assumption Made	Assumption Not Made
	X

QUESTION 5

Statement:

The students from Chile demanded that university education should be free. In 2012, they formed a protest around this topic.

Proposed Assumption:

Other universities outside Chile are free.

Assumption Made	Assumption Not Made
X	X

QUESTION 6

Statement:

The students from Chile demanded that university education should be free. In 2012, they formed a protest around this topic.

Proposed Assumption:

The Chilean students who protested had strong views regarding the price of university education.

Assumption Made	Assumption Not Made
✓	

QUESTION 7

Statement:

Lowering the age of consent means more girls will be at risk of being sexually abused and taken advantage of.

Proposed Assumption:

More girls will be at risk of being sexually abused if the age of consent was lowered.

Assumption Made	Assumption Not Made
✓	

QUESTION 8

Statement:

Lowering the age of consent means more girls will be at risk of being sexually abused and taken advantage of.

Proposed Assumption:

The age of consent has no impact on girls choosing to have sex, despite being underage.

Assumption Made	Assumption Not Made
	✗

QUESTION 9

Statement:

Lowering the alcohol limit for drivers means that drivers will be arrested if they do not change the amount of alcohol that they currently consume.

Proposed Assumption:

The alcohol limit needs to be lowered because there are considerably more accidents.

Assumption Made	Assumption Not Made
✗	✗

QUESTION 10

Statement:

Lowering the alcohol limit for drivers means that drivers will be arrested if they do not change the amount of alcohol that they currently consume.

Proposed Assumption:

Drivers are not currently being arrested for drink driving.

Assumption Made	Assumption Not Made
	✗

QUESTION 11

Statement:

The president claimed that he would prevent America from entering an economic crisis. However, in 2012, the country saw over 10 million USA citizens unemployed as a result of the economic depression.

Proposed Assumption:

Unemployment is an example of economic depression.

Assumption Made	Assumption Not Made
X	

QUESTION 12

Statement:

The president claimed that he would prevent America from entering an economic crisis. However, in 2012, the country saw over 10 million USA citizens unemployed as a result of the economic depression.

Proposed Assumption:

Presidents have an obligation to maintain their promises.

Assumption Made	Assumption Not Made
X	

QUESTION 13

Statement:

A business takes on a new employee. They are appointed as a programmer with a probation period of one year. Their performance will be reviewed in one year to discuss their future at the business.

Proposed Assumption:

A performance of an individual is generally not known when they are first employed.

Assumption Made	Assumption Not Made
X	

QUESTION 14

Statement:

A business takes on a new employee. They are appointed as a programmer with a probation period of one year. Their performance will be reviewed in one year to discuss their future at the business.

Proposed Assumption:

Their future at the business depends on their performance throughout the year.

Assumption Made	Assumption Not Made
X	

QUESTION 15

Statement:

A business takes on a new employee. They are appointed as a programmer with a probation period of one year. Their performance will be reviewed in one year to discuss their future as the business.

Proposed Assumption:

The employee will be guaranteed a permanent job position after their probation period is over.

Assumption Made	Assumption Not Made
X	X

QUESTION 16

Statement:

Apart from the entertainment purpose of television, its educational value cannot be disregarded.

Proposed Assumption:

Television only provides people with entertainment.

Assumption Made	Assumption Not Made
	X

QUESTION 17

Statement:

Apart from the entertainment purpose of television, its educational value cannot be disregarded.

Proposed Assumption:

The educational purpose is often overlooked.

Assumption Made	Assumption Not Made
X	

QUESTION 18

Statement:

Children are growing up in a world with significant influences and role models. Children spend large parts of their days at school and have become somewhat influenced by their teachers.

Proposed Assumption:

Children look up to their teachers as a role model.

Assumption Made	Assumption Not Made

QUESTION 19

Statement:

Children are at a vulnerable age where influences and role models are crucial. Children spend large parts of their days at school and have become somewhat influenced by their teachers.

Proposed Assumption:

Because of a child's age and their naïve manner, they are easily influenced and exposed to everything that happens around them.

Assumption Made	Assumption Not Made

QUESTION 20

Statement:

Inequality is a significant element of our social world. All existing inequalities can be reduced, maybe not be eradicated altogether but by active responses from the Government or revolutionary changes, inequality can be regulated.

Proposed Assumption:

Inequality is a man-made phenomenon.

Assumption Made	Assumption Not Made

QUESTION 21

Statement:

Inequality is a significant element of our social world. All existing inequalities can be reduced, maybe not be eradicated altogether but by active responses from the Government or revolutionary changes, inequality can be regulated.

Proposed Assumption:

The Government has made no effort so far in tackling the problem of inequality.

Assumption Made	Assumption Not Made
	X

QUESTION 22

Statement:

Lack of stimulation and encouragement at ages four and five can have adverse consequences.

Proposed Assumption:

A great deal of the development process happens in the early stages of childhood.

Assumption Made	Assumption Not Made
X	

QUESTION 23

Statement:

The health and safety rules and regulations play a vital role in any business. In India, the health and safety practices prove well below the international standard.

Proposed Assumption:

India do not comply with the international standard of health and safety rules and regulations within the work place.

Assumption Made	Assumption Not Made

QUESTION 24

Statement:

The health and safety rules and regulations play a vital role in any business. In India, the health and safety practices prove well below the international standard.

Proposed Assumption:

The health and safety rules and regulations in India businesses often comply with the international standard on health and safety procedures.

Assumption Made	Assumption Not Made

QUESTION 25

Statement:

There are many young male workers who have a manual labour job. Highly brilliant and compliant labourers are not always capable of expressing their knowledge and understanding through a verbal or written manner, instead they show their skills and knowledge in their work in a more practical way.

Proposed Assumption:

Manual labourers may not necessarily show levels of intellectual ability through written or verbal examinations, but can demonstrate a great 'hands-on' approach.

Assumption Made	Assumption Not Made

QUESTION 26

Statement:

There are many young male workers who have a manual labour job. Highly brilliant and compliant labourers are not always capable of expressing their knowledge and understanding through a verbal or written manner, instead they show their skills and knowledge in their work in a more practical way.

Proposed Assumption:

Manual labourers who do not like their job believe they would not be qualified or capable to do anything else.

Assumption Made	Assumption Not Made

QUESTION 27

Statement:

Fathers-to-be have the right to at least two weeks paid paternity leave. The Government have also introduced an Additional Paternity Leave whereby the parents are able to take six months off work, and receive the maternity pay that the mother would have got if she continued her maternity leave. This way both parents are able to enjoy the first 6 months off with their new-born.

Proposed Assumption:

Before the scheme for Additional Paternity Leave was introduced, fathers were unable to take paternity leave.

Assumption Made	Assumption Not Made

QUESTION 28

Statement:

Fathers-to-be have the right to at least two weeks paid paternity leave. The Government have also introduced an Additional Paternity Leave whereby the parents are able to take six months off work, and receive the maternity pay that the mother would have got if she continued her maternity leave. This way both parents are able to enjoy the first 6 months off with their new-born.

Proposed Assumption:

Fathers are entitled to at least two weeks of paternity leave and possibly more depending on circumstances and their employers.

Assumption Made	Assumption Not Made

QUESTION 29

Statement:

Due to divorce rates being high in the UK more and more custody cases are being filed in regards to which parent/guardian the child would be placed with. Depending on individual circumstances, the courts will choose the parent who will serve the child's best interests.

Proposed Assumption:

Every custody case is different.

Assumption Made	Assumption Not Made

QUESTION 30

Statement:

Due to divorce rates being high in the UK more and more custody cases are being filed in regards to which parent/guardian the child would be placed with. Depending on individual circumstances, the courts will choose the parent who will serve the child's best interests.

Proposed Assumption:

The courts always side with the mother and places the child in her custody.

Assumption Made	Assumption Not Made

RECOGNITION OF ASSUMPTIONS
TEST SECTION – ANSWERS

Q1.

Assumption made. For them to go by plane it must be possible to get a flight, so therefore this is necessarily assumed from the statement provided.

Q2.

Assumption made. It is assumed by the statement provided that going by plane is the quickest means of transportation compared to other transportation services, so therefore the assumption can be made.

Q3.

Assumption not made. It cannot be assumed that the only way to create compliant workers is through education.

Q4.

Assumption not made. The statement does not talk about students being unable to pay for university. The assumption is not referred to in the statement and therefore cannot be made.

Q5.

Assumption not made. The statement does not refer to other universities. The assumption to change university fees to being free of charge cannot be assumed.

Q6.

Assumption made. The statement refers to a student protest regarding university prices. This therefore assumes that the students had something to say and felt strongly about the issue.

Q7.

Assumption made. This assumption can be assumed from the statement provided that girls are more likely to be at risk of being abused if the age of consent is lowered.

Q8.

Assumption not made. The assumption proposed does not follow any logical explanation provided in the statement and therefore the assumption cannot be made.

Q9.

Assumption not made. This assumption cannot be made because it does not follow any logic given from the statement. The statement does not say anything about the number of accidents, so therefore this assumption does not follow.

Q10.

Assumption not made. The statement provided does not indicate whether drivers are currently being arrested or not, so therefore the assumption cannot be made.

Q11.

Assumption made. The statement indicates that unemployment rates is an example of economic depression so therefore the assumption can be made.

Q12.

Assumption not made. The statement does not provide any information regarding any obligation for presidents to maintain their promises. Therefore, this assumption cannot be made.

Q13.

Assumption made. The assumption suggests that it is difficult to determine a person's performance when they are first appointed and therefore this assumption can be made.

Q14.

Assumption made. It is assumed in the statement provided that the person's future will depend on their performance throughout their probation period of one year.

Q15.

Assumption not made. The statement shows no indication as to whether or not the new employee will be guaranteed a permanent job position at the end of their one year probation period. Therefore, the proposed assumption cannot be made.

Q16.

Assumption not made. The statement suggests that apart from entertainment, television also offers educational value, so therefore this assumption cannot be made.

Q17.

Assumption made. The statement suggests that its educational value cannot be disregarded and therefore suggests that it is often overlooked and ignored, so this assumption can be made.

Q18.

Assumption made. The statement suggests that a lot of influences on a child's life comes from their teachers so therefore this assumption can be presumed.

Q19.

Assumption made. It is assumed in the statement that children are at a vulnerable age and therefore, influences and role models are crucial. Therefore, the proposed assumption can be made.

Q20.

Assumption made. It is assumed in the statement that since inequality can be reduced, it is something we can fix, and therefore was something that we created. Therefore, the assumption can be made.

Q21.

Assumption not made. The statement does not indicate whether or not the Government have tried to tackle inequality in the past, so therefore the proposed assumption cannot be made.

Q22.

Assumption made. The statement suggests that ages four and five prove most significant in terms of being properly stimulated, so therefore the proposed assumption can be assumed.

Q23.

Assumption made. It is assumed from the statement provided that India do not comply with the international standards of health and safety practices enforced in the work place and therefore the assumption can be made.

Q24.

Assumption not made. The statement indicates that India does not comply with the international standard of health and safety procedures and instead are well below this standard, therefore this proposed assumption cannot be made.

Q25.

Assumption made. It can be assumed from the statement provided that manual labourers can express their skills and knowledge through a more 'hands-on' approach, rather than a written or verbal examination, so therefore this assumption can be made.

Q26.

Assumption not made. The statement does not indicate any thought or belief by any manual labourers on whether they like their jobs or not, so the proposed assumption cannot be made.

Q27.

Assumption not made. The assumption does not follow logically from the statement provided. The statement shows no indication or claim that fathers were unable to take time off and therefore this assumption cannot be made.

Q28.

Assumption made. It can be assumed from the statement provided that fathers are now entitled to at least two weeks paternity leave, so therefore this assumption can be made.

Q29.

Assumption made. It is assumed that this is a reasonable assumption to make due to the statement indicating that individual circumstances vary and therefore will depend on the outcome.

Q30.

Assumption not made. It cannot be assumed from the statement provided that the courts always side with the mother. The statement does not say anything about the statistical rate in which the courts side with either parent and therefore the proposed assumption cannot be made.

CHAPTER 3

Deduction

In this chapter, you will focus on the term **deduction**. Deduction is a way of eliminating the wrong answers from the right one. The aim of this test is to demonstrate your level of critical thinking and how you interpret the information you are provided with.

For this test, you need to carefully read through each statement and conclusion and work out whether the conclusion can be made from the previous statement. For these statements, you need to take them at face value. Consider each statement as true, regardless of what you believe. You need to try and not let your personal judgement interfere with your answers. You need to answer based only on the information you are provided with and not what you know to be true.

Here is an example of the type of question you are likely to face in the deduction section of the BCAT.

> **Statement:** A new business opens up. New companies are far more likely to struggle and fail as opposed to businesses that have been up and running for years.

> **Conclusion:** Businesses that have been up and running for years are far more profitable than a new company that has only been around for a couple of years.

The example suggests that most new businesses are likely to fail. However you cannot draw the conclusion that businesses that have been up and running for years will have better profits. There is no data to prove whether or not a well-established business is financially stronger. Therefore this **conclusion does not follow.**

In this chapter, you will be provided with 30 sample questions. You will be given a statement which you are to regard as true. For each statement, you will then be given a possible conclusion. You will have to work through each question and determine whether you think the conclusion follows on from the statement provided or whether it does not.

Please note that we have purposely not provided you with a time limit. You should work through these questions slowly and carefully, to ensure you understand what is expected, and how to answer the questions correctly.

HOW TO ANSWER THE QUESTION

For each statement, you will be given a choice of 2 possible answers: **Conclusion Follows** and **Conclusion Does Not Follow.**

You must tick the box which seems most accurate and reasonable.

ANSWER OPTIONS

Tick **Conclusion Follows** if you believe the conclusion does follow on from the statement and therefore provides a logical outcome.

Tick **Conclusion Does Not Follow** if you think that the conclusion does not necessarily follow on from the statement and therefore provides an illogical overview of the facts provided.

EXAMPLE 1

Statement:

Workers are either practical or theoretical. If people are practical, they are not theoretical.

Proposed Conclusion:

All employees are practical based or theoretical based.

Conclusion Follows	Conclusion Does Not Follow
✓	

Answer Example 1 – Feedback:

From the statement provided, it describes two types of employees – practical and theoretical. Therefore this conclusion does follow because it suggests that employees have to be either theoretical or practical based.

EXAMPLE 2

Statement:

Walks in the rain are always fun. You get to jump in puddles. Puddles make me happy.

Proposed Conclusion:

Walks in the sunshine are boring.

Conclusion Follows	Conclusion Does Not Follow
	✓

Answer Example 2 – Feedback:

This conclusion does not follow. You cannot tell from the statement whether sunny walks are boring or not. Some walks in the sunshine may be fun. Therefore, you cannot draw upon this conclusion from the statement provided.

DEDUCTION TESTING QUESTIONS

QUESTION 1

Statement:

Workers are either practical or theoretical. If people are practical, they are not theoretical.

Proposed Conclusion:

It is impossible for a person to be theoretical if they are already practical.

Conclusion Follows	Conclusion Does Not Follow
X	

QUESTION 2

Statement:

Workers are either practical or theoretical. If people are practical, they are not theoretical.

Proposed Conclusion:

Jack works in design, therefore he must be practical.

Conclusion Follows	Conclusion Does Not Follow
	X

QUESTION 3

Statement:

Companies are expanding their presence on the web. Most companies believe that in order to succeed they should devote more time in web designing and SEO. However, it is obvious that companies are more likely to succeed if they pay attention to data management and social networking.

Proposed Conclusion:

Only companies that devote their time in social networking and data management will succeed.

Conclusion Follows	Conclusion Does Not Follow
	✗

QUESTION 4

Statement:

Companies are expanding their presence on the web. Most companies believe that in order to succeed they should devote more time in web designing and SEO. However, it is obvious that companies are more likely to succeed if they pay attention to data management and social networking.

Proposed Conclusion:

No company is spending time on web design and SEO.

Conclusion Follows	Conclusion Does Not Follow
	✗

QUESTION 5

Statement:

Companies are expanding their presence on the web. Most companies believe that in order to succeed they should devote more time in web designing and SEO. However, it is obvious that companies are more likely to succeed if they pay attention to data management and social networking.

Proposed Conclusion:

Data management is more important than web design.

Conclusion Follows	Conclusion Does Not Follow
✗	

QUESTION 6

Statement:

People in poverty suffer multiple physical illnesses. All people in poverty with multiple physical illnesses are unhappy.

Proposed Conclusion:

People who are happy are not poor.

Conclusion Follows	Conclusion Does Not Follow

QUESTION 7

Statement:

People in poverty suffer multiple physical illnesses. All people with multiple physical illnesses are unhappy.

Proposed Conclusion:

Some people who are poverty stricken are happy.

Conclusion Follows	Conclusion Does Not Follow

QUESTION 8

Statement:

Many people receive income support. Some people pay working taxes.

Proposed Conclusion:

There are more people who receive income support than people who pay their taxes.

Conclusion Follows	Conclusion Does Not Follow
	X

QUESTION 9

Statement:

Many people receive income support. Some people pay working taxes.

Proposed Conclusion:

People who receive income support do not work.

Conclusion Follows	Conclusion Does Not Follow
	X

QUESTION 10

Statement:

You get nervous when being interviewed. Everyone who gets interviewed feels apprehensive.

Proposed Conclusion:

If you are not apprehensive, you won't be nervous.

Conclusion Follows	Conclusion Does Not Follow
	X

QUESTION 11

Statement:

You get nervous when being interviewed. Everyone who gets interviewed feels apprehensive.

Proposed Conclusion:

If you are being interviewed, you are going to feel nervous and apprehensive.

Conclusion Follows	Conclusion Does Not Follow

QUESTION 12

Statement:

Some winters it is snowy. Some snowy days are fun.

Proposed Conclusion:

No snowy day is boring.

Conclusion Follows	Conclusion Does Not Follow

QUESTION 13

Statement:

Cigarettes cause many problems. Cigarettes always cause health damage. Cigarettes cause damage to the environment.

Proposed Conclusion:

Cigarettes cause damage to both health and the environment.

Conclusion Follows	Conclusion Does Not Follow

QUESTION 14

Statement:

Cigarettes cause many problems. Cigarettes always cause health damage. Cigarettes cause damage to the environment.

Proposed Conclusion:

If you are healthy, it means that you do not smoke.

Conclusion Follows	Conclusion Does Not Follow

QUESTION 15

Statement:

Most films are not boring. A lot of the films show some level of violence.

Proposed Conclusion:

Every film is violent.

Conclusion Follows	Conclusion Does Not Follow

QUESTION 16

Statement:

Most films are not boring. A lot of the films show some level of violence.

Proposed Conclusion:

Most films that do not contain violence are boring.

Conclusion Follows	Conclusion Does Not Follow

QUESTION 17

Statement:

Some lawyers become judges in the future of their legal careers. All lawyers argue on behalf of their clientele before standing up in front of a jury.

Proposed Conclusion:

Every lawyer becomes a judge.

Conclusion Follows	Conclusion Does Not Follow

QUESTION 18

Statement:

Some lawyers become judges in the future of their legal careers. All lawyers argue on behalf of their clientele before standing up in front of a jury.

Proposed Conclusion:

If a lawyer is successful, it means they would have a successful career as a judge.

Conclusion Follows	Conclusion Does Not Follow

QUESTION 19

Statement:

Some weekends it is sunny. All sunny days are happy.

Proposed Conclusion:

No rainy day is happy.

Conclusion Follows	Conclusion Does Not Follow

QUESTION 20

Statement:

Some weekends it is sunny. All sunny days are happy.

Proposed Conclusion:

Not every weekend is sunny.

Conclusion Follows	Conclusion Does Not Follow

QUESTION 21

Statement:

The police were investigating a murder. They were interviewing a witness. The witness claimed that John had blood over his hands and ran off from where the incident happened.

Proposed Conclusion:

The witness saw John commit murder.

Conclusion Follows	Conclusion Does Not Follow

QUESTION 22

Statement:

The police were investigating a murder. They were interviewing a witness. The witness claimed that John had blood over his hands and ran off from where the incident happened.

Proposed Conclusion:

The police have spoken to John in relation to the murder.

Conclusion Follows	Conclusion Does Not Follow

QUESTION 23

Statement:

Each book I have seen in the university library is more than a year old. I go into the library every week.

Proposed Conclusion:

Every book in the library is over a year old.

Conclusion Follows	Conclusion Does Not Follow

QUESTION 24

Statement:

Each book I have seen in the university library is more than a year old. I go into the library every week.

Proposed Conclusion:

The person who goes into the library every week has seen most of the books the library has.

Conclusion Follows	Conclusion Does Not Follow

QUESTION 25

Statement:

Most religious people go to church. People who go to church pray, wash away their sins or go there for some peace.

Proposed Conclusion:

Only religious people go to church.

Conclusion Follows	Conclusion Does Not Follow

QUESTION 26.

Statement:

Most religious people go to church. People who go to church pray, wash away their sins or go there for some peace.

Proposed Conclusion:

Every person who goes to church, goes there to pray.

Conclusion Follows	Conclusion Does Not Follow

QUESTION 27

Statement:

Alcoholism causes health damage. Alcoholism effects the people you care about.

Proposed Conclusion:

Alcoholism causes health damage or effects your relationships with the people you care about.

Conclusion Follows	Conclusion Does Not Follow

QUESTION 28

Statement:

Alcoholism causes health damage. Alcoholism effects the people you care about.

Proposed Conclusion:

Alcoholics do not care about their health.

Conclusion Follows	Conclusion Does Not Follow

QUESTION 29

Statement:

Most people believe TV shows are there to serve the purpose of entertainment. However, some entertainment shows are there for educational purposes also.

Proposed Conclusion:

Television shows only serve the purpose of entertainment.

Conclusion Follows	Conclusion Does Not Follow

QUESTION 30

Statement:

Most people believe TV shows are there to serve the purpose of entertainment. However, some entertainment shows are there for educational purposes also.

Proposed Conclusion:

All entertainment shows provide educational purposes.

Conclusion Follows	Conclusion Does Not Follow

DEDUCTION - ANSWERS

Q1.

Conclusion follows. It is stated in the sentence that if people are practical, they are not going to be theoretical. Therefore the conclusion follows in that a person cannot be theoretical if they are already practical.

Q2.

Conclusion does not follow. This generalises the statement. We cannot know from Jack's occupation of working in design whether or not he is practical or theoretical, we could assume it would most likely be practical and 'hands on', but that is a significant assumption to make.

Q3.

Conclusion does not follow. The use of the word 'only' makes the conclusion false. The use of the words 'far more likely' means a possibility, it is not set in stone, and therefore the conclusion cannot follow.

Q4.

Conclusion does not follow. Again, this conclusion cannot follow the statement. The statement does not mention anything in regards to what other companies are spending their time on.

Q5.

Conclusion does not follow. You cannot tell whether data management is more important than web design. The statement uses both data management and social networking to compare web design and SEO. You cannot tell which one is more important based on the four options stated.

Q6.

Conclusion follows. If poor people equates to unhappiness, then the opposite is happy people are people who are not poor. Therefore the conclusion does follow.

Q7.

Conclusion does not follow. The use of the word 'some' is a way to determine existence. The statement does not mention anything about poverty in relation to happiness, therefore you cannot draw this conclusion.

Q8.

Conclusion does not follow. There is no way to indicate how many people pay taxes and how many people receive income support. Therefore the conclusion cannot follow.

Q9.

Conclusion does not follow. You cannot tell from the information provided whether or not people who get income support work, therefore this conclusion cannot follow.

Q10.

Conclusion does not follow. It is impossible to say how people feel when they are not being interviewed, so the conclusion is too much of a generalised statement.

Q11.

Conclusion follows. The statement provides the case of 'if this, then this'. Therefore if you are nervous, you are going to be apprehensive, therefore the conclusion does follow.

Q12.

Conclusion does not follow. You cannot tell from the statement whether or not all snowy days are fun, some might not be, and therefore this conclusion cannot be drawn.

Q13.

Conclusion follows. The use of the word 'both' means that it causes health damage and environmental damage. It doesn't cause either or, therefore the conclusion follows.

Q14.

Conclusion follows. The statement follows the formalisation of 'if this, then this'. Smoke equals health damage, therefore this equivalent to no smoking equals no health damage. Therefore the conclusion follows.

Q15.

Conclusion does not follow. The statement indicates that 'most' films are not boring as 'a lot' of films contain some violence. It does not mention that 'every' film is violent, therefore this conclusion cannot be concluded from the statement provided.

Q16.

Conclusion does not follow. We cannot infer the extent to which boring and violence overlap, therefore this conclusion cannot be drawn.

Q17.

Conclusion does not follow. The use of the word 'some' refers to only some of the judges, therefore you cannot conclude that 'every' lawyer will become a judge and so the conclusion does not follow.

Q18.

Conclusion does not follow. The statement does not mention anything about the success rate in comparison to lawyers and judges, and therefore the conclusion cannot be drawn on from the statement provided.

Q19.

Conclusion does not follow. You cannot tell from the statement whether rainy days are happy or not. Therefore you cannot make this conclusion.

Q20.

Conclusion follows. The use of the word 'some' in the statement means that not every weekend will be sunny, so therefore the conclusion does follow from the statement provided.

Q21.

Conclusion does not follow. The statement does not mention anything about whether or not the witness saw John commit murder, therefore this conclusion cannot be drawn.

Q22.

Conclusion does not follow. You are not provided with any information in regards to whether the police have spoken to John, therefore you cannot make this conclusion.

Q23.

Conclusion does not follow. You cannot tell based on how many books a person has seen whether all the books are a year old. That person may have missed a book that is less than a year old, therefore this conclusion cannot be drawn.

Q24.

Conclusion does not follow. You cannot tell how many books the person has actually seen. Just because the person goes into the library every week, it doesn't mean they look at all the types of books there are, they may have a preference. Therefore this conclusion cannot be drawn.

Q25.

Conclusion does not follow. The statement does not mention anything about non-religious people going to church, they might well do. Therefore this conclusion does not follow.

Q26.

Conclusion does not follow. The statement gives three possibilities of reasons people go to church. They don't all go there for all three, therefore not every person goes there to pray so the conclusion does not follow.

Q27.

Conclusion does not follow. The statement indicates that alcoholism affects both your health and the people who care about you. Therefore the conclusion saying it affects either or, cannot be concluded.

Q28.

Conclusion does not follow. The statement does not mention anything about what alcoholics care about. They might care about their health but simply have a problem of giving up alcohol. Therefore this conclusion cannot be concluded.

Q29.

Conclusion does not follow. The statement indicates that both entertainment and educational purposes should be considered in regards to TV shows, therefore this conclusion does not follow.

Q30.

Conclusion does not follow. The use of the word 'some' in the statement means that only some of the entertainment shows provide a level of education. Therefore, you cannot conclude that 'all' entertainment shows serve an educational purpose.

CHAPTER 4

Interpretation

In this chapter, you will focus on the term **interpretation.** Interpretation is a way of explaining the meaning of something. You need to be able to show that you can critically engage with a passage or information, and interpret the information to form a solid conclusion.

For this test, you need to carefully read through each statement and then read each proposed conclusion. You will need to determine whether the proposed conclusion you are given follows on from the statement provided. In other words, can the conclusion be reached from what you have just read? For these statements, you are to regard them as true. You need to try and not let your own prejudice interfere with your answers in order to provide accurate results.

Here is an example of the type of question you are likely to face in the interpretation section of the BCAT.

> **Statement:** A study of patterns and colours was taken with children from the ages eight months to 5 years. The study showed that children responded to certain colours and patterns and suggests that they react to certain patterns, colours and images.

> **Conclusion:** Children from an early age begin the learning process which is seen through their reactions to particular colours, patterns and pictures.

This example demonstrates a **conclusion that follows** on from the statement. In the statement you are told of the children's reactions in regards to colours and patterns. The conclusion draws upon this information and concludes the information, therefore showing that the conclusion does follow on.

In this chapter, you will be provided with 30 sample questions. You will be given a statement which you are to regard as true. For each statement, you will then be given a possible conclusion. You will have to interpret each question one by one and determine whether you think the conclusion follows on from the statement provided or whether it does not.

Please note that we have purposely not provided you with a time limit. You should work through these questions slowly and carefully, to ensure you understand what is expected, and how to answer the questions correctly.

HOW TO ANSWER THE QUESTION

For each statement, you will be given a choice of 2 possible answers: **Conclusion Follows** and **Conclusion Does Not Follow**.

You must tick the box which seems most accurate and reasonable.

ANSWER OPTIONS

Tick **Conclusion Follows** if you believe the conclusion does follow on from the statement and therefore provides a logical outcome.

Tick **Conclusion Does Not Follow** if you think that the conclusion does not necessarily follow on from the statement and therefore provides an illogical overview of the facts provided.

EXAMPLE 1

Statement:

A company was looking at ways to cut expenses. In an attempt to do so, the business let go of their advertising department and outsourced their advertising needs from an advertising company. This would allow the company to save 25% for the year on its advertising expenses.

Proposed Conclusion:

The aim of the company's advertising outsourcing, was so the business could earn more profits.

Conclusion Follows	Conclusion Does Not Follow
	✓

Answer Example 1 – Feedback:

The conclusion does not follow on from the statement provided. Although it could be assumed that the business wants to earn more profits, it is not stated as a reason as to why the business wants to save money, so therefore this conclusion cannot be drawn.

EXAMPLE 2

Statement:

A new fashion company is opening. It is often said that new companies are more likely to fail in the first two years of opening as opposed to well-established companies that have been around for several years.

Proposed Conclusion

The new fashion company is going to fail.

Conclusion Follows	Conclusion Does Not Follow
	✓

Answer Example 2 – Feedback:

Although the statement suggests that new companies are more likely to fail, it cannot predict that the new fashion company will fail. Therefore the conclusion cannot be drawn from the statement provided.

INTERPRETATION TESTING QUESTIONS

QUESTION 1

Statement:

A company was looking for ways to cut expenses. In an attempt to do so, the business let go of their advertising department and outsourced their advertising needs from an advertising company. This would allow the company to save 25% for the year on its advertising expenses.

Proposed Conclusion:

The company has been able to save ¼ of their advertising expenditures by outsourcing their advertising requirements.

Conclusion Follows	Conclusion Does Not Follow
✓	

QUESTION 2

Statement:

A company was looking for ways to cut expenses. In an attempt to do so, the business let go of their advertising department and outsourced their advertising needs from an advertising company. This would allow the company to save 25% for the year on its advertising expenses.

Proposed Conclusion:

The company saved 25% by outsourcing one of their departments. If other companies were to do the same, they too would save money.

Conclusion Follows	Conclusion Does Not Follow
	✗

QUESTION 3

Statement:

A new fashion company is opening. It is often said that new companies are more likely to fail in the first two years of opening as opposed to well-established companies that have been around for several years.

Proposed Conclusion:

Well-established companies will not fail or close down.

Conclusion Follows	Conclusion Does Not Follow

QUESTION 4

Statement:

A new fashion company is opening. It is often said that new companies are more likely to fail in the first two years of opening as opposed to well-established companies that have been around for several years.

Proposed Conclusion:

Well-established companies stand a bigger chance of succeeding as opposed to newer companies that struggle in their first two years of opening.

Conclusion Follows	Conclusion Does Not Follow

QUESTION 5

Statement:

The South East and Central Southern England had a record rainfall of 175.2 mm in January 2014 – beating the previous record of 158.2 mm in 1988. Predictions of rainfall and weather conditions are often inaccurate and prove extremely difficult to predict the outcome.

Proposed Conclusion:

The rainfall in 2014 was not predicted by weather forecasters.

Conclusion Follows	Conclusion Does Not Follow

QUESTION 6

Statement:

The South East and Central Southern England had a record rainfall of 175.2 mm in January – beating the previous record of 158.2 mm in 1988. Predictions of rainfall and weather conditions are often inaccurate and prove extremely difficult to predict the outcome.

Proposed Conclusion:

The rainfall in 1988 for South East and Central Southern England was less than that of 2014.

Conclusion Follows	Conclusion Does Not Follow

QUESTION 7

Statement:

Every responsible leader has to face making difficult decisions. However, some leaders dislike the idea of having to make complex decisions and facing tough choices.

Proposed Conclusion:

Irresponsible leaders avoid making difficult decisions because they do not like to make them.

Conclusion Follows	Conclusion Does Not Follow

QUESTION 8

Statement:

Every responsible leader has to face making difficult decisions. However, some leaders dislike the idea of having to make complex decisions and facing tough choices.

Proposed Conclusion:

Some responsible leaders make tough choices despite not liking the idea of making complex decisions.

Conclusion Follows	Conclusion Does Not Follow

QUESTION 9

Statement:

A beauty store takes pride in producing some of the finest and most natural beauty products on the market. Free from animal testing, these beauty products are free from parabens, sulfates, mineral oils and chemical toxins in order to provide natural and organic beauty.

Proposed Conclusion:

The store's products are unlikely to contain any man-made setting agents.

Conclusion Follows	Conclusion Does Not Follow

QUESTION 10

Statement:

A study of children suggests that the first two years of a child's life is a crucial stage of child development. It is important to engage your child with an environment in which they are able to learn from, especially in regards to language. Singing to your child, talking and reading will provide the essential foundation for a child's vocational abilities in order to develop.

Proposed Conclusion:

If you teach your child great language skills from an early age, your child will develop quicker in regards to walking.

Conclusion Follows	Conclusion Does Not Follow

QUESTION 11

Statement:

A study of children suggests that the first two years of a child's life is a crucial stage of child development. It is important to engage your child with an environment in which they are able to learn from, especially in regards to language. Singing to your child, talking and reading will provide the essential foundation for a child's vocational abilities in order to develop.

Proposed Conclusion:

Singing and talking to a child is a crucial step in child development.

Conclusion Follows	Conclusion Does Not Follow

QUESTION 12

Statement:

A press conference is taking place in France. Staff are asked to travel by train unless the journey time or cost is 4% more than going by plane, and in that case they can go by plane.

Proposed Conclusion:

If a staff member travels by plane but it costs the same as going by train, the journey time must be 4% shorter than going by plane.

Conclusion Follows	Conclusion Does Not Follow

QUESTION 13

Statement:

A press conference is taking place in France. Staff are asked to travel by train unless the journey time is 4% more than going by plane, and in that case they can go by plane.

Proposed Conclusion:

Staff are asked to travel by train for convenient purposes.

Conclusion Follows	Conclusion Does Not Follow

QUESTION 14

Statement:

A press conference is taking place in France. Staff are asked to travel by train unless the journey time is 4% more than going by plane, and in that case they can go by plane.

Proposed Conclusion:

Staff are only allowed to go by plane if it is the cheapest means of transportation.

Conclusion Follows	Conclusion Does Not Follow

QUESTION 15

Statement:

Two witnesses claimed a man committed a knife crime. The man's fingerprints are all over the knife. The police are using this evidence as their main lead.

Proposed Conclusion:

The fingerprints of the man make him a prime suspect.

Conclusion Follows	Conclusion Does Not Follow

QUESTION 16

Statement:

It has snowed in Massachusetts every December for the last 50 decades.

Proposed Conclusion:

It will snow in Massachusetts this December.

Conclusion Follows	Conclusion Does Not Follow

QUESTION 17

Statement:

The New York Public Library is one of the largest libraries in the United States. It holds nearly 53 million items.

Proposed Conclusion:

The New York Public Library may not be the largest library in the United States.

Conclusion Follows	Conclusion Does Not Follow

QUESTION 18

Statement:

The New York Public Library is one of the largest libraries in the United States. It holds nearly 53 million items.

Proposed Conclusion:

The New York Public Library is larger than the libraries in the UK.

Conclusion Follows	Conclusion Does Not Follow

QUESTION 19

Statement:

The financial sector has become difficult to regulate. Bankers are no longer seen as reliable or trustworthy and executives of financial institutions are often seen as overpaid.

Proposed Conclusion:

The general public have never trusted the financial sector.

Conclusion Follows	Conclusion Does Not Follow

QUESTION 20

Statement:

The financial sector has become difficult to regulate. Banks are no longer seen as reliable or trustworthy and executives of financial institutions are often seen as overpaid.

Proposed Conclusion:

Overpaid executives of the financial sector could be seen as an underlying problem as to why the financial sector is difficult to regulate.

Conclusion Follows	Conclusion Does Not Follow

QUESTION 21

Statement:

Economists argue that individuals and firms in the private sector are better at creating jobs for themselves and spark economic growth. They produce higher profit incentives and political popularity to ensure efficiency.

Proposed Conclusion:

The private sector work alongside the public sector to ensure efficiency.

Conclusion Follows	Conclusion Does Not Follow

QUESTION 22

Statement:

Economists claim that individuals and firms in the private sector are better at creating jobs for themselves and spark economic growth. They produce higher profit incentives and political popularity to ensure efficiency.

Proposed Conclusion:

Economists are against the private sector.

Conclusion Follows	Conclusion Does Not Follow

QUESTION 23

Statement:

Economists claim that individuals and firms in the private sector are better at creating jobs for themselves and spark economic growth. They produce higher profit incentives and political popularity to ensure efficiency.

Proposed Conclusion:

The private sector is a useful way to ensure higher incentives and effective results.

Conclusion Follows	Conclusion Does Not Follow

QUESTION 24

Statement:

Firefighters have issued further strikes in regards to pension proposals. The current proposal means workers can be dismissed at the age of 60 because they cannot maintain physical fitness requirements. The new proposal hopes for firefighters to be able to retire at a more flexible age of 55 and still keep their pension schemes.

Proposed Conclusion:

The Government currently have the opportunity to dismiss firefighters at an older age because of their physical fitness not being up to the required standard.

Conclusion Follows	Conclusion Does Not Follow

QUESTION 25

Statement:

Firefighters have issued further strike in regards to pension proposals. The current proposal means workers can be dismissed at the age of 60 because they cannot maintain physical fitness requirements. The new proposal hopes for firefighters to be able to retire at a more flexible age of 55 and still keep their pension schemes.

Proposed Conclusion:

Firefighters are inadequate of doing their job properly at the age of 60.

Conclusion Follows	Conclusion Does Not Follow

QUESTION 26

Statement:

Firefighters have issued further strike in regards to pension proposals. The current proposal means workers can be dismissed at the age of 60 because they cannot maintain physical fitness requirements. The new proposal hopes for firefighters to be able to retire at a more flexible age of 55 and still keep their pension schemes.

Proposed Conclusion:

The new proposal hopes to improve the opportunities of firefighters by letting them retire at a more reasonable age and ensure their pension is not affected.

Conclusion Follows	Conclusion Does Not Follow

QUESTION 27

Statement:

A police Constable speaks out on the police force's aims and objectives. He claims to "make our neighbourhood a secure and safe environment. We act as a channel of communication – passing on information and data from our service to the general public to help detect and protect our community from crime".

Proposed Conclusion:

The neighbourhood has a lot of crimes.

Conclusion Follows	Conclusion Does Not Follow

QUESTION 28

Statement:

A police Constable speaks out on the police force's aims and objectives. He claims to "make our neighbourhood a secure and safe environment. We act as a channel of communication – passing on information and data from our service to the general public to help detect and protect our community from crime".

Proposed Conclusion:

The police act as a device to ensure information and data is received and delivered between the service they provide and the public.

Conclusion Follows	Conclusion Does Not Follow

QUESTION 29

Statement:

The jury are responsible for deciding whether or not the facts that are presented to them, determine if a person can be found guilty or not guilty of the offence for which they have been charged.

Proposed Conclusion:

The jury interprets the law in their own way.

Conclusion Follows	Conclusion Does Not Follow

QUESTION 30

Statement:

The jury are responsible for deciding whether the facts that are presented to them, a person can be found guilty or not guilty of the offence for which they have been charged.

Proposed Conclusion:

The jury have the final say in regards to sentencing a person.

Conclusion Follows	Conclusion Does Not Follow

INTERPRETATION – ANSWERS

Q1.

Conclusion follows. The company has saved 25% on their advertising requirements by outsourcing the advertising department to a local advertising company. So, their 25% (1/4) of the business's expenditures have been saved, so therefore the conclusion follows from the statement provided.

Q2.

Conclusion does not follow. The statement does not indicate that other businesses could prosper by outsourcing one of their departments. The statement only talks about the company's profits, it is by no means of a way to indicate the prosperities of other companies, so therefore the conclusion does not follow.

Q3.

Conclusion does not follow. The statement talks about the difference between new companies and well-established companies. It does not indicate any possibility that well-established companies will not fail. This cannot be assumed from the statement provided, so therefore the conclusion does not follow.

Q4.

Conclusion follows. The statement suggests that new companies are more likely to fail as opposed to well-established companies. The conclusion follows in that it demonstrates how well-established companies have a better chance of succeeding and surviving in comparison to newer companies.

Q5.

Conclusion does not follow. The statement shows no indication of whether or not the forecasters were able to predict the rainfall of 2014 correctly. Therefore, the conclusion cannot be drawn from the statement provided.

Q6.

Conclusion follows. The statement suggests that the rainfall in January 2014 was greater than the rainfall in 1988, which clearly illustrates that the conclusion follows on from the statement provided.

Q7.

Conclusion does not follow. From the statement provided, you cannot draw the conclusion that every irresponsible leader avoids making difficult decisions, simply because they do not like to make them. Irresponsible leaders may make those tough choices and get on with making decisions, so therefore this conclusion does not follow.

Q8.

Conclusion follows. The conclusion emphasises the word "some". "Some" leaders do not like to make difficult decisions, but they make them anyway. The conclusion follows in that the statement claims that whilst some leaders do not like the idea of making difficult choices, "some" of them get on with it and do it. So therefore the conclusion does follow the statement provided.

Q9.

Conclusion follows. The beauty products are meant to be "natural products". Therefore, this conclusion can be made because the statement indicates that their beauty products are made from organic and natural substances and therefore are unlikely to contain any man-made setting agent.

Q10.

Conclusion does not follow. The statement does not say anything about walking in relation to language and vocational ability, therefore you cannot draw upon this conclusion.

Q11.

Conclusion follows. It can be concluded from the statement provided that early vocabulary and language skills play a significant role in the child development process, so therefore this conclusion follows.

Q12.

Conclusion follows. The statement reinforces that staff are permitted to go by plane if the journey time or cost is 4% less than that by going by train. Therefore this conclusion follows.

Q13.

Conclusion does not follow. The statement does not suggest any reason as to why the staff are asked to travel by train. It may have been for convenience, it may be for environmental purposes or other reasons, therefore this conclusion cannot be drawn.

Q14.

Conclusion does not follow. The statement does not say anything about cost, so therefore this conclusion cannot be drawn.

Q15.

Conclusion follows. The police are using the evidence of the fingerprints as their main lead. This reinforces that their main lead is the man whose fingerprints they belong to, therefore this conclusion can be drawn.

Q16.

Conclusion does not follow. It cannot be predicted that it will snow in Massachusetts this December despite the last 50 years doing so, therefore this conclusion cannot be drawn.

Q17.

Conclusion follows. The statement claims that the New York Public Library is 'one' of the largest libraries in the US. It does not mean that it is the largest. Therefore the conclusion follows.

Q18.

Conclusion does not follow. The statement does not mention anything about UK libraries, so therefore you are unable to determine whether the NY library is larger than libraries in the UK, and thus this conclusion does not follow.

Q19.

Conclusion does not follow. The statement says that bankers are 'no longer' seen as reliable. So, therefore, the conclusion does not state that bankers have 'never' been trusted, thus the conclusion does not follow.

Q20.

Conclusion follows. The statement indicates that banks are no longer seen as reliable and that executives are being overpaid. So it is possible to say that this could be why the financial sector is difficult to regulate.

Q21.

Conclusion does not follow. The statement does not say anything about the public sector, so you cannot determine whether or not they work alongside one another to ensure efficiency, so therefore the conclusion cannot be drawn.

Q22.

Conclusion does not follow. The statement does not show any indication of what economists believe about the private sector, therefore this conclusion cannot be drawn.

Q23.

Conclusion follows. The statement gives the reasons of higher incentives as a way of ensuring efficiency, so therefore this conclusion can be drawn.

Q24.

Conclusion follows. The government have the right to dismiss workers for these reasons as stated in the passage, and therefore this conclusion does follow.

Q25.

This conclusion cannot follow because it is a generalisation. The statement does not claim whether or not all firefighters are still capable of doing their job at the age of 60, so therefore the conclusion cannot be drawn.

Q26.

Conclusion follows. The statement indicates the aims of the new proposal and how it can help workers retire at a more reasonable age in order to ensure their pension is not affected.

Q27.

Conclusion does not follow. Despite the aims and objectives given by the Constable, there is no data or information to suggest whether the neighbourhood has a lot of crime. Therefore this conclusion cannot be drawn.

Q28.

Conclusion follows. The conclusion follows on from the statement given by displaying the intentions of the police force and how they act as a communication device for the general public, therefore this conclusion can be drawn.

Q29.

Conclusion does not follow. The role of the jury is to take into consideration all the evidence and data of a court case. They do not interpret the law themselves, therefore this conclusion cannot be drawn.

Q30.

Conclusion does not follow. The statement does not say anything about whether the jury has the final judgement in the case. Although you might know from knowledge that the judge has the final say, that is not mentioned, so therefore the conclusion cannot follow from the statement provided.

CHAPTER 5

Evaluation of Arguments

In this chapter, you will focus on **Evaluation of Arguments.** The role of a barrister is to make important decisions and distinguish between strong and weak arguments, data and evidence. This is exactly what this test will entail.

For each question, you will be presented with either a statement or question which you are to regard as fact. You will then be given a proposed argument. This proposed argument will either agree or disagree with what has been said. The difficulty comes next, in which you must read each proposed argument carefully and identify whether it is a strong or weak argument.

For example, you may be given the statement below:

> Should speed cameras be a compulsory safety requirement along every main road in the UK in order to reduce the amount of road accidents?

This acts as your statement; you will now be given a proposed argument:

> No, having speed cameras along every main road in the UK makes the neighbourhoods look unsafe.

Your task is to determine whether the above proposed argument is valid or not. Does it present a significant argument? Does it directly relate to the question? This proposed conclusion is **weak**. Although it mentions the action (putting speed cameras in place), it does not refer to the consequences of the action (reducing car accidents). The argument mentions neighbourhoods looking unsafe; this does not have anything to do with the roads 'being' unsafe. You cannot arrive at this conclusion based on opinion and logical explanation, you are solely to base your answer on the information you are given!

In this chapter, you will be provided with 30 sample questions. You should regard each argument and statement to be true. For each statement/ argument, you will then be given a possible argument. For the purpose of this test, you will need to interpret each argument and decide whether the argument being presented is strong or weak.

Please note that we have purposely not provided you with a time limit. You should work through these questions slowly and carefully, to ensure you understand what is expected, and how to answer the questions correctly.

HOW TO ANSWER THE QUESTION

For each statement, you will be given a choice of 2 possible answers: **Argument Strong** and **Argument Weak**.

ANSWER OPTIONS

Tick **Argument Strong** if you believe the argument is both significant and direct in relation to the question.

Tick **Argument Weak** if you think that the argument is not strong enough to work. If it does not directly relate to the question, or only shows minor importance or relativity to the argument, you are to regard the argument as weak.

EXAMPLE 1

Statement:

Should speed cameras be a compulsory safety requirement along every main road in the UK in order to reduce the amount of road accidents?

Proposed Argument:

Yes, speeding has become a huge factor in the safety of driving. Speed cameras have proven to reduce the amount of road accidents and help improve the safety of drivers on the road.

Argument Strong	Argument Weak
✓	

Answer Example 1 – Feedback:

This argument provides solid reasoning and directly links back to the statement provided. The first part of the argument mentions one of the main reasons for road accidents. Secondly, the argument mentions how the speed cameras can be used to reduce road accidents and improve road safety. Therefore, these parts of the argument combined, make a **strong**, valid and important argument.

EXAMPLE 2

Statement:

Should speed cameras be a compulsory safety requirement along every main road in the UK in order to reduce the amount of road accidents?

Proposed Argument:

No, not all road accidents are caused by dangerous driving.

Argument Strong	Argument Weak
	✓

Answer Example 2 – Feedback:

This proposed argument is a **weak argument**. There is no relation from the argument and the actual statement. Although it does mention the consequences of unsafe driving in terms of road accidents, there is no link to speed cameras. The argument mentions 'dangerous driving'. The statement does not indicate anything about dangerous driving, in fact there may be a number of reasons for road accidents, and therefore this argument alone is not reason enough to reject speed cameras.

EVALUATION OF ARGUMENTS TESTING QUESTIONS

QUESTION 1

Statement:

Should parents encourage their children to participate in extra activities and learning programmes, in order to reach their full learning potential?

Proposed Argument:

Yes, parents have the responsibility to help their children succeed in whatever they want to do in life.

Argument Strong	Argument Weak

QUESTION 2

Statement:

Should parents encourage their children to participate in extra activities and learning programmes, in order to reach their full learning potential?

Proposed Argument:

Yes, extra activities and learning programmes are a great way for children to reach their full learning ability. They will be provided with useful skills, knowledge and talents that will help them develop in their learning process.

Argument Strong	Argument Weak

QUESTION 3

Statement:

Should parents encourage their children to participate in extra activities and learning programmes, in order to reach their full learning potential?

Proposed Argument:

No, children who want to learn will do so. Children do not want to feel pressurised in doing something they might end up resenting their parents for. Children will develop in their own time and in their own way.

Argument Strong	Argument Weak

QUESTION 4

Statement:

Should the Government allow convicted criminals the right to expunge their criminal record after 5 years of being sentenced?

Proposed Argument:

No, the Government will be blamed if the convicted criminals commit any further crime.

Argument Strong	Argument Weak

QUESTION 5

Statement:

Should the Government allow convicted criminals the right to expunge their criminal record after 5 years of being sentenced?

Proposed Argument:

Yes, everyone has the right for a second chance.

Argument Strong	Argument Weak

QUESTION 6

Statement:

Should the Government allow convicted criminals the right to expunge their criminal record after 5 years of being sentenced?

Proposed Argument:

Yes, allowing expulsion of criminal records will allow convicted criminals the opportunity to become rehabilitated and adjust better in society.

Argument Strong	Argument Weak

QUESTION 7

Statement:

Should schools provide free school dinners for every student?

Proposed Argument:

Yes, providing free school dinners for every student will help to ensure students are eating a healthy and balanced meal every day.

Argument Strong	Argument Weak

QUESTION 8

Statement:

Should schools provide free school dinners for every student?

Proposed Argument:

No, the Government is spending too much on expenses and therefore cannot afford to lose out on money.

Argument Strong	Argument Weak

QUESTION 9

Statement:

Should university be free for every student?

Proposed Argument:

No, making university free for every student will make too many highly qualified people, and there are not enough jobs.

Argument Strong	Argument Weak

QUESTION 10

Statement:

Should university be free for every student?

Proposed Argument:

Yes, having more highly qualified workers will ensure businesses with high level candidates who will bring productivity and knowledge to the organisation.

Argument Strong	Argument Weak

QUESTION 11

Statement:

Should the Government provide extra financial support to parents with children under the age of six to ensure a better standard of living?

Proposed Argument:

Yes, providing extra financial support for parents who have children under the age of six will allow a better quality start in life for children who are at a crucial stage of development.

Argument Strong	Argument Weak

QUESTION 12

Statement:

Should the Government provide extra financial support to parents with children under the age of six to ensure a better standard of living?

Proposed Argument:

No, the Government are already in financial difficulty.

Argument Strong	Argument Weak

QUESTION 13

Statement:

Should the Government provide extra financial support to parents with children under the age of six to ensure a better standard of living?

Proposed Argument:

No, the Government already provide benefits for parents and families that need it. Providing more financial support could jeopardise society; considering more people are having babies, the Government would not be able to keep up the support for long and therefore society would be in financial crisis.

Argument Strong	Argument Weak

QUESTION 14

Statement:

Should it be compulsory for every student to go on to higher education?

Proposed Argument:

No, a lot of people do not have the will power or interest in going on to higher education. These people lose motivation and are unable to focus. Making them go on to higher education would be a waste of their time and their teachers.

Argument Strong	Argument Weak

QUESTION 15

Statement:

Should it be compulsory for every student to go on to higher education?

Proposed Argument:

No, everyone should have the right to choose their own career path. Some people are not interested in academics and therefore would excel in something they are actually interested in and want to pursue.

Argument Strong	Argument Weak

QUESTION 16

Statement:

Should it be compulsory for every student to go on to higher education?

Proposed Argument:

Yes, making higher education compulsory will allow them to experience the 'crazy' college life.

Argument Strong	Argument Weak

QUESTION 17

Statement:

Should people under the age of 16 be allowed to vote?

Proposed Argument:

No, people under the age of 16 have little knowledge on political goings-on and therefore would not be able to fully appreciate or comprehend their actions in regards to their vote.

Argument Strong	Argument Weak

QUESTION 18

Statement:

Should people under the age of 16 be allowed to vote?

Proposed Argument:

Yes, people under the age of 16 who are not allowed to vote feel left out.

Argument Strong	Argument Weak

QUESTION 19

Statement:

Should all employees be given the opportunity to work flexi-hours?

Proposed Argument:

Yes, employees should be given the opportunity to work flexi-hours if it improves their home/work life and provides a more happy, productive and flexible approach.

Argument Strong	Argument Weak

QUESTION 20

Statement:

Should all employees be given the opportunity to work flexi-hours?

Proposed Argument:

No, employees will be given flexibility and are likely to take advantage of it.

Argument Strong	Argument Weak

QUESTION 21

Statement:

Should the drinking age in the UK be lowered to 16?

Proposed Argument:

No, lowering the drinking age in the UK to 16 is likely to cause more damage than good. These youngsters are vulnerable, inexperienced and immature and therefore will not know the harm of alcohol and its possible repercussions.

Argument Strong	Argument Weak

QUESTION 22

Statement:

Should the drinking age in the UK be lowered to 16?

Proposed Argument:

Yes, 16 year olds drink alcohol anyway, 16 years old look older than they are and can get away with it.

Argument Strong	Argument Weak

QUESTION 23

Statement:

Should employers who are employing candidates use the candidates Facebook and Twitter pages as part of their selection process?

Proposed Argument:

No, employers should find out about the candidates themselves and not base their judgements on statuses and images. An objective impression cannot be made in the case of using social networking as a way of getting to know someone.

Argument Strong	Argument Weak

QUESTION 24

Statement:

Should employers who are employing candidates use the candidates Facebook and Twitter pages as part of their selection process?

Proposed Argument:

No, employers have no right to 'stalk' and intrude on the candidate's personal life by searching their Facebook and Twitter pages.

Argument Strong	Argument Weak

QUESTION 25

Statement:

Should psychologists be made to come forward if a patient of theirs has admitted to committing a crime?

Proposed Argument:

No, psychologists who break client confidentiality means the patient will no longer feel secure and trusting and therefore will not confide or want to stay in the rehabilitation process.

Argument Strong	Argument Weak

QUESTION 26

Statement:

Should psychologists be made to come forward if a patient of theirs has admitted to committing a crime?

Proposed Argument:

No, it is no business of the psychologist to get involved with such matters.

Argument Strong	Argument Weak

QUESTION 27

Statement:

Should it be a compulsory school lesson for students to learn first aid and health care?

Proposed Argument:

Yes, teaching first aid and health care to students will provide them with vital information that could come in useful in the future. They are more likely to feel competent and aware about situations if they are taught them from an early age, therefore being more productive in the future.

Argument Strong	Argument Weak

QUESTION 28

Statement:

Should it be a compulsory school for students to learn first aid and health care?

Proposed Argument:

No, if students take no interest in the lesson, they will not pay attention to what is being told anyway.

Argument Strong	Argument Weak

QUESTION 29

Statement:

Should students be made to take religious studies at school?

Proposed Argument:

No, there is little benefit of teaching religious studies if they don't believe in it, or if they believe in something other than what is being taught. Religion cannot be inflicted on people; it is something you either believe in or don't. So teaching children who do not want to learn about religion is unproductive and unbeneficial.

Argument Strong	Argument Weak

QUESTION 30

Statement:

Should students be made to take religious studies at school?

Proposed Argument:

Yes, everyone should be engaged with different religions in our world.

Argument Strong	Argument Weak

EVALUATION OF ARGUMENTS – ANSWERS

Q1.

Argument weak. This argument lacks the direct link back to the statement in question. The statement identifies extra activities and learning programmes as possible ways in which their children can reach their full learning potential. However, the argument does not mention these possible ways to achieve success, and 'help them to achieve whatever' seems a little vague in terms of children reaching their maximum learning potential.

Q2.

Argument strong. The argument links directly back to the statement. It talks about the examples of extra activities and learning programmes as a way of increasing a child's learning abilities. The argument also gives ways in which it can help reach their potential through learning new skills and talents, which provides a solid argument for parents to encourage their children.

Q3.

Argument strong. The argument targets both the action being presented and the consequences of their actions. It states that parents shouldn't encourage their children to participate in such programmes and activities and gives reasons as to why. This links back to the initial action of getting parents to encourage their children and giving clear and concise examples as to why they shouldn't.

Q4.

Argument weak. The argument does not focus on the expunging of criminal records. Instead, it focuses on criminals committing other crimes. Although it does provide an example of the consequences in terms of the Government, the overall argument provides trivial details and therefore does not provide a strong argument.

Q5.

Argument weak. This argument does not offer any insight into the initial statement provided. There is no clear link between the statement and the argument. The argument only works on beliefs and emotions. There is no solid ground to work with in terms of a valid argument. The argument mentions second chances; it does not refer to the expunging of criminal records and therefore there is missing information in this argument which makes it weak.

Q6.

Argument strong. The argument shows a clear link between the statement provided and the proposed argument. The argument mentions the supposed action (expunging of criminal records) and the possible consequences that could take place in relation to the action. It relates the action to a positive effect which it could have, therefore producing an important and strong argument.

Q7.

Argument strong. The argument refers to the action (providing school dinners) and links it directly to the positive effect that it will enable students to be given a healthy and balanced meal every day. This is a solid and reasonable argument to make which links directly back to the statement.

Q8.

Argument weak. There is no clear link between the statement and the proposed conclusion. Although the conclusion talks about a possible negative effect (the Government are spending too much money and cannot afford it); it does not however link back to the notion of implementing free school dinners. Therefore, it does not provide a significant argument.

Q9.

Argument weak. The argument only addresses two possible issues (highly qualified people and lack of jobs). However the argument does not discuss these issues any further and therefore does not provide a strong and valid argument.

Q10.

Argument strong. The argument provides a positive that would come out of making university free for every student (creating more highly qualified workers) and discusses it further to show how it would benefit a company (by bringing productivity and knowledge). Therefore, this argument provides strong reasoning.

Q11.

Argument strong. The argument not only refers back to the initial statement (in regards to extra financial support for parents with children under the age of six) but it also gives reason as to how it can help children develop in their most crucial stages of childhood, and so it provides a strong argument.

Q12.

Argument weak. This argument is extremely weak in that it lacks a clear and concise argument in regards to the statement. It provides no evidence or reasoning. It just claims the government are already in financial difficulty, the argument doesn't mention how this would not provide any benefits.

Q13.

Argument strong. The argument provides a clear and concise argument. It provides a statement as to why the government shouldn't provide extra financial support, it gives reasons why and explains the implications if they did. Therefore, it provides a strong and valid argument.

Q14.

Argument strong. The argument is a strong argument because it gives reasoning and examples as to how it would not benefit some people who are not suited to the role of school and academia.

Q15.

Argument strong. This argument is strong and valid. It gives clear and concise reasons as to why higher education should not be made compulsory and gives further examples of how people can excel in something they actually want to do, rather than feel pressured to do it.

Q16.

Argument weak. This would be an inappropriate and meaningless reason as to why higher education should be made compulsory. It provides no real significance and is somewhat irrelevant, and therefore is a weak argument.

Q17.

Argument strong. The argument provides a solid and valid argument which gives not only a reason, but the importance of that reason and its impact, which is all linked back to statement in question.

Q18.

Argument weak. This is no reason to base an argument on. It provides little significance, if any and therefore makes the argument weak. The argument needs to have more detail, reasoning and examples to back up the statement, so therefore this argument does not work.

Q19.

Argument strong. The argument gives a reason to back up the idea of implementing flexi-hours and gives examples as to how employees will benefit from it, therefore it provides a valid argument which can be deemed important and strong.

Q20.

Argument weak. Although the argument gives a valid reason as to why employees should not be given flexi-hour opportunities, it is not backed up. It is based merely on assumption, and assumptions are not strong enough to base an argument on.

Q21.

Argument strong. The argument provides reasonable logic which is backed up by a clear statement against lowering the age to 16 for drink. It gives clear examples as to why it should not be lowered and gives possible implications, therefore it ties in and links back to the statement, which makes it a strong argument.

Q22.

Argument weak. Although the argument does give some reason as to why the drinking age should be lowered, the reason 'because they already get away with it' is not strong enough to work as an argument. The argument needs more logical explanation and support to make the argument work.

Q23.

Argument strong. This is a strong argument which relates directly back to the statement. It gives evidence, examples and reasoning which, all together works to form this solid argument.

Q24.

Argument weak. Although this provides a reasonable statement as to why employers should not use a person's Facebook and Twitter page, it does not explain it further. It is based on someone's belief or opinions which cannot form a solid argument without support.

Q25.

Argument strong. The argument focuses on both the action (forcing psychologists to come forward if a patient admits to any unlawful crimes) and the consequences it has on either the person or society (the patient will lose the feeling of trust and security and no longer continue their rehabilitation process).

Q26.

Argument weak. The argument presents no clear or valid explanation as to why psychologists should not get involved. The argument needs more clarity and structure. It needs examples and consequences in regards to getting involved.

Q27.

Argument strong. The argument links clearly back to the reason and benefits it would have if health care and first aid were made compulsory school lessons. The argument gives explanations and examples of the benefits it would bring on both themselves and society.

Q28.

Argument weak. This argument provides little significance. It does not work because there is no clear explanation or reasoning and it is not supported. It is based on a person's general opinion and therefore provides no clear and concise argument.

Q29.

Argument strong. The argument gives clear examples and explanations as to why students should not be made to take religious studies. It gives the possible effects of teaching religion and gives a clear understanding as to its impracticality.

Q30.

Argument weak. Although the argument gives a reasonable statement as to why religious studies should be taught in schools, it does not expand it any further. It does not go on to say the benefits of teaching religion or how this would impact people or society, so therefore it does not provide a strong enough argument.

CHAPTER 6

The Bar Course Aptitude Test Mock Test

So, you have worked through the previous chapters and answered all the questions. Do you think you are ready to take your BCAT? Give it a try! This chapter is designed to help give you an idea of what to expect when you sit your BCAT.

This mock test for the Bar Course Aptitude Test is based on everything you have previously learned throughout the book. The test will be laid out in a similar way to what you can expect in the real BCAT in order to fully prepare yourself.

You will be given 60 questions and you will have 55 minutes to answer all the questions. Time is very limited, so you have to make sure that you answer all the questions with speed, but without losing accuracy!

Try your best to stick to the time limit. It will be great practice for when you come to sit your real test, and this way you will be able to work on your timing skills!

The test will include all five of the chapters you have previously completed. To give you a quick reminder, here are the five elements of the Bar Course Aptitude Test:

1. Inference
2. Recognition of Assumptions
3. Deduction
4. Interpretation
5. Evaluation of Arguments

The mock test will work as followed. You will be given instructions which you should read before you begin your test. It will state exactly what you have to do, your time limit and the number of questions you will have to answer.

(Note: reading the instructions and examples is also included in your 55 minute time limit, so make sure you take that into consideration!)

You will then be given several examples for which you will be shown how they are worked out and the reasons behind the answer (just like the beginning of the previous chapters). You will then need to complete the questions that follow. Once you have completed the section, you will then be given several examples of how to answer the next lot of questions and so forth.

After you have completed your mock test, use the scoring system in chapter 7 to work out whether you passed. You will be given one of three possible scores:

1. Pass
2. Marginal fail
3. Significant fail

Note: please be aware that we cannot give you an exact number of how many marks you will need to pass the BCAT. The number of exact marks is not available, but is claimed by the Bar Standards Board that the grade boundary to pass is set quite low; and the majority of candidates do pass. The pass mark is set quite low in order to find strong candidates and who will more likely succeed at the BPTC.

You should carefully consider your score and determine whether you have what it takes to progress in your training of becoming a barrister. The real test is just one small step for becoming a barrister. If you really struggled and scored a significant fail, you may want to practice more before sitting your real test or you may want to weigh up your options as to whether a career as a barrister is right for you.

Good luck.

BCAT MOCK TEST

BAR COURSE APTITUDE TEST (BCAT)

In this test, you will be tested on your abilities to show critical thinking and judgements regarding certain scenarios.

There are 5 test sections, each of which will have their own instructions and examples. You should read through this carefully to ensure you know exactly how to proceed in regards to answering the questions.

For each question, you will be given a statement. Your job is to determine which answer seems most logical and appropriate.

Your score will depend solely on the number of questions you have answered correctly, so it is imperative that you try to answer every question, even if you are unsure about the correct answer.

The test includes 60 questions. You will have a time limit of 55 minutes, which includes reading through the instructions, example questions and the test itself.

If you finish before the allotted time is up, you should read back through your answers and make sure you answered them as best you could.

You will then be given a scoring sheet. You will either score a 'pass', 'marginal fail' or a 'significant fail'. If you failed, look back through your answers and try to work out where you went wrong and what you need to do differently.

Good luck!

BAR COURSE APTITUDE TEST (BCAT)
TEST SECTION 1: INFERENCE

INSTRUCTIONS

An inference is a conclusion that can be drawn from the facts or supposed facts of a given statement.

For example, if lights are left on in a house, you could infer that someone was home. However, not all inferences are true or can be justified. The lights may be on because the people who live there want people to believe someone is home, even though this might not be the case.

For this section, you will be given a statement that you are to assume to be true, despite knowledge or belief otherwise. You will be given a conclusion that you might be able to draw from upon the facts provided.

Your task is to determine whether the inference being stated can be drawn from the statement.

For each inference, you will be given 5 possible choices in which you can answer:

True – if the inference is definitely true; it follows reasonable logic and does not contradict the statement in any way.

Probably True – if the inference is more than likely to be true; it is not definite but it is probably true and follows some reasonable logic and clarity.

Insufficient Data – if there is no evidence or data to back it up, then the inference cannot be made.

Probably False – if the inference is more than likely to be false; it is not definitely false but it is probably false.

False – if the inference is definitely false; it follows no logic or is wrong or contradicts the statement in some way.

INFERENCE - EXAMPLE 1

Statement:

A study of children between the ages of 8 months and 6 years old were studied in regards to their language. The study indicates that children are at their most significant developing stages. Research claims that children who learn more than 1 language or sign language from an early age have better brain development. Multilingualism is proven to enhance your child's education and helps develop better reading and writing skills.

Proposed Inference:

Multilingualism will ensure your child grows up speaking more than one language fluently.

True	Probably True	Insufficient Data	Probably False	False
		✓		

Feedback: There is no evidence to suggest that children who speak different languages from an early age continue with the language in order to become a fluent speaker.

INFERENCE - EXAMPLE 2

Statement:

A study of children between the ages of 8 months and 6 years old were studied in regards to their language. The study indicates that children are at their most significant developing stages. Research claims that children who learn more than 1 language or sign language from an early age have better brain development. Multilingualism is quite often proven to enhance your child's education and develop better reading and writing skills.

Proposed Inference:

Learning multiple languages as a child, helps their brain development.

True	Probably True	Insufficient Data	Probably False	False
✓				

Feedback: the statement claims that brain development is better when a child learns multiple languages therefore the inference is true.

Now it's your turn!

QUESTION 1

Statement:

A parent went into a school and demanded a meeting with the headmaster. She sat there and complained about the lack of action regarding anti-social behaviour. She claimed that her son was being bullied when a boy in the year above pulled his seat out from beneath him. The headmaster emphasised the importance of distinguishing between behaviour that is typical 'boy banter', harmless fun and behaviour that was inappropriate and victimising.

Proposed Inference:

The headmaster did not classify the behaviour of pulling out the child's seat from beneath him as bullying.

True	Probably True	Insufficient Data	Probably False	False
	X			

QUESTION 2

Statement:

A parent went into a school and demanded a meeting with the headmaster. She sat there and complained about the lack of action regarding anti-social behaviour. She claimed that her son was being bullied when a boy in the year above pulled his seat out from beneath him. The headmaster emphasised the importance of distinguishing between behaviour that is typical 'boy banter', harmless fun and behaviour that was inappropriate and victimising.

Proposed Inference:

There are no procedures in place at the school to tackle anti-social behaviour.

True	Probably True	Insufficient Data	Probably False	False
		X		

QUESTION 3

Statement:

A parent went into a school and demanded a meeting with the headmaster. She sat there and complained about the lack of action regarding anti-social behaviour. She claimed that her son was being bullied when a boy in the year above pulled his seat out from beneath him. The headmaster emphasised the importance of distinguishing between behaviour that is typical 'boy banter', harmless fun and behaviour that was inappropriate and victimising.

Proposed Inference:

His mother was so angry because her son got hurt from the incident.

True	Probably True	Insufficient Data	Probably False	False
	X			

QUESTION 4

Statement:

The smoking ban was brought in to the UK to stop people from smoking in public places i.e. restaurants, pubs, workplaces etc. Martin believes the legislation is a breach of his human rights and privacy. Martin was given an £80 fine for smoking on three different occasions in the space of a one month period.

Proposed Inference:

Martin believes that any contradicting law that interferes with human rights should be broken.

True	Probably True	Insufficient Data	Probably False	False
	X			

QUESTION 5

Statement:

The smoking ban was brought in to the UK to stop people from smoking in public places i.e. restaurants, pubs, workplaces etc. Martin believes the legislation is a breach of his human rights and privacy. Martin was given an £80 fine for smoking on three different occasions in the space of a one month period.

Proposed Inference:

There was at least one week during the month which Martin did not get fined for smoking in a public place.

True	Probably True	Insufficient Data	Probably False	False
X				

QUESTION 6

Statement:

The smoking ban was brought in to the UK to stop people from smoking in public places i.e. restaurants, pubs, workplaces etc. Martin believes the legislation is a breach of his human rights and privacy. Martin was given an £80 fine for smoking on three difference occasions in the space of a one month period.

Proposed Inference:

Martin believes the right to privacy and being able to smoke where and when you want is more important than the health of other people which he is smoking around.

True	Probably True	Insufficient Data	Probably False	False
		X	X	

QUESTION 7

Statement:

A hundred students attend the National Gallery in London. The Gallery has over 2,300 masterpieces which range from the late medieval era to contemporary art and sculptures.

Proposed Inference:

The hundred students that attended the National Gallery were Art students.

True	Probably True	Insufficient Data	Probably False	False
	X			

X

QUESTION 8

Statement:

A woman has recently given birth to twins – a boy and a girl. Her first week home she sets them into a routine. She knows around 5pm, her son begins to cry because it is his feeding time.

Proposed Inference:

Its 5'oclock. It will be her son that is going to cry.

True	Probably True	Insufficient Data	Probably False	False
	X			

QUESTION 9

Statement:

A bank got robbed in the early hours of Saturday morning. There were 8 hostages, 3 of them being employees at the bank. A man in a balaclava pointed a gun at one of the bankers and demanded the money from her till. She handed the money to the man in the balaclava at the same time he was tackled from behind by one of the hostages. A gunshot went off.

Proposed Inference:

The banker who handed over the money was a man.

True	Probably True	Insufficient Data	Probably False	False
				X

QUESTION 10

Statement:

A bank got robbed in the early hours of Saturday morning. There were 8 hostages, 3 of them being employees at the bank. A man in a balaclava pointed a gun at one of the bankers and demanded the money from her till. She handed the money to the man in the balaclava at the same time he was tackled from behind by one of the hostages. A gunshot went off.

Proposed Inference:

The man who tackled the man in the balaclava was shot.

True	Probably True	Insufficient Data	Probably False	False
		X		

QUESTION 11

Statement:

A bank got robbed in the early hours of Saturday morning. There were 8 hostages, 3 of them being employees at the bank. A man in a balaclava pointed a gun at tone of the bankers and demanded the money from her till. She handed the money to the man in the balaclava at the same time he was tackled from behind by one of the hostages. A gunshot went off.

Proposed Inference:

The man in the balaclava escaped the bank with the money from the till.

True	Probably True	Insufficient Data	Probably False	False
			X	

QUESTION 12

Statement:

Urban areas of the UK, particularly in London are often associated with crime. Violence is one way of being able to express people's views. The Government are trying to tackle issues of gang related crime which are often linked with disadvantaged neighbourhoods, adolescence and lack of opportunities.

Proposed Inference:

Gang related crime is also associated with ethnic and cultural backgrounds.

True	Probably True	Insufficient Data	Probably False	False
		X		

BAR COURSE APTITUDE TEST (BCAT)
TEST SECTION 2: RECOGNITION OF ASSUMPTIONS

INSTRUCTIONS

Recognising assumptions can often be tricky. An assumption is something that we presume to be true, or something we take for granted. For example, if someone were to say that they were graduating in September, you can assume that the person passed their university degree and therefore are eligible to graduate.

For this section, you will be given a statement that you are to assume to be true, despite knowledge or belief otherwise. For each statement, you will be given a possible assumption. In other words, you will need to work out whether the statement is really making that assumption. Note that assumptions may not always be justifiable or factual, you cannot judge these assumptions based on common knowledge. You are to take the assumptions at face value and determine whether the assumption can be made.

For each assumption, you will be given a statement or passage to read, you will answer either:

Tick **assumption made** is you believe that an assumption can be made by the facts provided.

Tick **assumption not made** if you think that an assumption cannot be made by the facts provided.

ASSUMPTION - EXAMPLE 3

Statement:

Many trainee managers are university graduates. Businesses claim that graduates are far more likely to make the transition into that position much quicker as opposed to non-graduate candidates.

Proposed Assumption:

Non-graduate candidates are unable to fulfil the position of trainee manager.

Assumption Made	Assumption Not Made
	✓

Feedback: the statement does not indicate that non-graduates are 'unable' to fulfil the position, they may be more than capable. The statement suggests graduates are 'more' likely to make the transition into that role much quicker, therefore this assumption cannot be made.

ASSUMPTION - EXAMPLE 4

Statement:

Many trainee managers are university graduates. Businesses claim that graduates are far more likely to make the transition into that position much quicker as opposed to non-graduate candidates.

Proposed Assumption:

If a business wants to employ someone who is going to make the transition into that role quickly, they are more likely to go for a university graduate.

Assumption Made	Assumption Not Made
✓	

Feedback: From the statement, it was clearly indicated that businesses who employ graduates will progress quicker into that role, so therefore it can be assumed that they are far more likely to employ a graduate if they were looking for someone who will progress more quickly.

Now it's your turn!

QUESTION 13

Statement:

A physician tells a middle aged lady that eating a plum a day helps control heart rate and blood pressure. Plums have plenty of minerals like potassium and iron, which are essential components for a healthy body.

Proposed Assumption:

It can be believed that the middle aged lady either has a problem with her heart rate or her blood pressure.

Assumption Made	Assumption Not Made
X	

QUESTION 14

Statement:

A physician tells a middle aged lady that eating a plum a day helps control heart rate and blood pressure. Plums have plenty of minerals like potassium and iron, which are essential components for a healthy body.

Proposed Assumption:

Your blood pressure will increase after eating a plum.

Assumption Made	Assumption Not Made
	X

QUESTION 15

Statement:

Members of staff who lack respect and don't get along with their colleagues, suggests employers were unsuccessful in picking the right candidates.

Proposed Assumption:

Common courtesy amongst employees helps to demonstrate that the employers were successful in staff recruitment.

Assumption Made	Assumption Not Made
X	

QUESTION 16

Statement:

Members of staff who lack respect and don't get along with their colleagues, suggests employers were unsuccessful in picking the right candidates.

Proposed Assumption:

Courtesy issues creates lack of work ethic and motivation.

Assumption Made	Assumption Not Made
X	

QUESTION 17

Statement:

Members of staff who lack respect and don't get along with their colleagues, suggests employers were unsuccessful in picking the right candidates.

Proposed Assumption:

Employer success can be defined through their staff management.

Assumption Made	Assumption Not Made
	X

QUESTION 18

Statement:

Celebrities have become an increasingly influential factor concerning children of today. Celebrities have a responsibility, despite not agreeing to it, to set an example for children; who often grow up influenced by a celebrity role model of their choice.

Proposed Assumption:

Celebrity role models are the reason for children's aggressive behaviour.

Assumption Made	Assumption Not Made
	X

QUESTION 19

Statement:

Celebrities have become an increasingly influential factor concerning children of today. Celebrities have a responsibility, despite not agreeing to it, to set an example for children; who often grow up influenced by a celebrity role model of their choice.

Proposed Assumption:

It is believed that celebrities have more of an impact today than in the past.

Assumption Made	Assumption Not Made
X	

QUESTION 20

Statement:

If continuous rainfall persists in certain areas of the UK, precautions will need to be taken. The South of the UK need to be ready to deal with torrential rainfall. Ensuring their homes are protected from flooding and to ensure homes that lose power and heating; a quick route to fixing the problem is important.

Proposed Assumption:

All of the UK need to prepare for torrential rainfall.

Assumption Made	Assumption Not Made
	X

QUESTION 21

Statement:

If continuous rainfall persists in certain areas of the UK, precautions will need to be taken. The South of the UK need to be ready to deal with torrential rainfall. Ensuring their homes are protected from flooding and to ensure homes that lose power and heating; a quick route to fixing the problem is important.

Proposed Assumption:

If we are to expect torrential rainfall, precautions will need to be taken in regards to gardens and other landscapes.

Assumption Made	Assumption Not Made
	X

QUESTION 22

Statement:

If continuous rainfall persists in certain areas of the UK, precautions will need to be taken. The South of the UK need to be ready to deal with torrential rainfall. Ensuring their homes are protected from flooding and to ensure homes that lose power and heating; a quick route to fixing the problem is important.

Proposed Assumption:

The South of the UK need to be ready to take precautionary action if torrential rainfall continues.

Assumption Made	Assumption Not Made

QUESTION 23

Statement:

Research studies suggest that the chlorogenic acid found in blueberries helps to lower blood sugar levels and control blood glucose levels in type II diabetes.

Proposed Assumption:

Blueberries are the only way to monitor and control lowering blood sugar levels.

Assumption Made	Assumption Not Made

QUESTION 24

Statement:

Research studies suggest that the chlorogenic acid found in blueberries helps to lower blood sugar levels and control blood glucose levels in type II diabetes.

Proposed Assumption:

If you have high blood sugar levels, eating blueberries might help to lower your blood sugar level.

Assumption Made	Assumption Not Made

BAR COURSE APTITUDE TEST (BCAT)
TEST SECTION 3: DEDUCTION

INSTRUCTIONS

In this section to test Deduction, you will be given a premise/statement and a conclusion. The aim is to identify whether or not the conclusion follows.

For the purpose of this test, you must consider each premise as true. Whether this is unjustified, or in your personal belief to be wrong, you should regard each statement to be true without exception.

For example, if you were told that all bread is fresh, you need to take it as 'all', even mouldy bread is fresh. Obviously, you know this would not be the case, but for the purpose of this test, you need to take it at face value.

For each deduction exercise, you will be given a statement or passage to read, you will answer either:

Conclusion Follows – If you think that the conclusion follows on from the statement and forms some logic.

Conclusion Does Not Follow – If you think that the conclusion does not necessarily follow on from the statement, despite your personal judgement and general knowledge to believe it to be true.

DEDUCTION - EXAMPLE 5

Statement:

Overweight people suffer from multiple health issues and/or illnesses. All people with an illness or health issue suffer with some form of depression.

Proposed Conclusion:

People who are healthy do not suffer with some form of depression.

Conclusion Follows	Conclusion Does Not Follow
✓	

Feedback: Conclusion follows. The statement suggests overweight equals health issues; health issues equals depression. Meaning healthy people equal contented.

DEDUCTION – EXAMPLE 6

Statement:

Overweight people suffer from multiple health issues and/or illnesses. All people with an illness or health issue suffer with some form of depression.

Proposed Conclusion:

Health issues and illnesses are the consequences of being overweight.

Conclusion Follows	Conclusion Does Not Follow
	✓

Feedback: the statement does not mention whether or not being ill or having some form of health problem is the direct consequence of being overweight.

Now it's your turn!

QUESTION 25

Statement:

An employer is looking for a candidate to fulfil a managerial role. He is looking for someone who is ambitious. Everyone who is ambitious is motivated to succeed and do well in their careers.

Proposed Conclusion:

Success comes from being ambitious and motivated.

Conclusion Follows	Conclusion Does Not Follow
	✗

QUESTION 26

Statement:

An employer is looking for a candidate to fulfil a managerial role. He is looking for someone who is ambitious. Everyone who is ambitious is motivated to succeed and do well in their careers.

Proposed Conclusion:

If someone is motivated, they do not always show themselves to be ambitious.

Conclusion Follows	Conclusion Does Not Follow
	✗

QUESTION 27

Statement:

An employer is looking for a candidate to fulfil a managerial role. He is looking for someone who is ambitious. Everyone who is ambitious is motivated to succeed and do well in their careers.

Proposed Conclusion:

Every managerial role, regardless of the employer, requires ambition.

Conclusion Follows	Conclusion Does Not Follow

QUESTION 28

Statement:

People with an alcoholic problem suffer health issues. Alongside health issues, they also experience psychological issues.

Proposed Conclusion:

Every alcoholic who experiences health issues also experiences psychological problems.

Conclusion Follows	Conclusion Does Not Follow

QUESTION 29

Statement:

People with an alcoholic problem suffer health issues. Alongside health issues, they also experience psychological issues.

Proposed Conclusion:

Alcoholics who experience psychological problems always feel some form of social anxiety.

Conclusion Follows	Conclusion Does Not Follow

QUESTION 30

Statement:

All candidates are either a leader or a follower. Only people who lack leadership lack confidence.

Proposed Conclusion:

If a candidate is a 'leader', they will have confidence.

Conclusion Follows	Conclusion Does Not Follow
X	

QUESTION 31

Statement:

All candidates are either a leader or a follower. Only people who lack leadership lack confidence.

Proposed Conclusion:

Candidates who are 'followers' do as they are told.

Conclusion Follows	Conclusion Does Not Follow
	X

QUESTION 32

Statement:

Some children suffer with dyslexia. All children with dyslexia show some level of social anxiety.

Proposed Conclusion:

Children with dyslexia struggle in school.

Conclusion Follows	Conclusion Does Not Follow

QUESTION 33

Statement:

Some children suffer with dyslexia. All children with dyslexia show some level of social anxiety.

Proposed Conclusion:

Children with dyslexia progress slower than children without dyslexia.

Conclusion Follows	Conclusion Does Not Follow

QUESTION 34

Statement:

Some children suffer with dyslexia. All children with dyslexia show some level of social anxiety.

Proposed Conclusion:

Social anxiety is one of the symptoms of suffering with dyslexia.

Conclusion Follows	Conclusion Does Not Follow

QUESTION 35

Statement:

Research shows that children that grow up without a father suffer more psychological problems. All psychological problems in children will affect their attitude and behaviour when growing up.

Proposed Conclusion:

Children with a father do not suffer any psychological problem.

Conclusion Follows	Conclusion Does Not Follow

QUESTION 36

Statement:

Research shows that children that grow up without a father suffer more psychological problems. All psychological problems in children will affect their attitude and behaviour when growing up.

Proposed Conclusion:

Psychological problems are a common issue for children without a father.

Conclusion Follows	Conclusion Does Not Follow

BAR COURSE APTITUDE TEST (BCAT)
TEST SECTION 4: INTERPRETATION

INSTRUCTIONS

Interpretation is the way in which something can be interpreted in order to form a conclusion.

For the purpose of this test, you must consider each premise/passage to be true. Whether this is unjustified, or in your personal belief to be wrong, you should regard each statement to be true without exception.

For example, if you are told that every December it snows, even if you don't believe this or you know this to be wrong, for the sole purpose of this test, you are to base your answer on regarding the statement as fact.

For each interpretation exercise, you will be given a statement or passage to read, you will answer either:

Conclusion Follows – If you think that the conclusion follows on from the statement and forms logical explanation.

Conclusion Does Not Follow – If you think that the conclusion does not necessarily follow on from the statement, despite your personal judgement and general knowledge to believe it to be true.

Now it's your turn!

INTERPRETATION – EXAMPLE 7

Statement:

Children who have autistic tendencies may suffer with repetitive body movements such as rocking, pacing or hand flapping. Many autistic children suffer relatively delayed responses and therefore this affects their development process.

Proposed Conclusion:

People will know if a child has autistic tendencies because they will show signs of repetitive rocking.

Conclusion Follows	Conclusion Does Not Follow
	✓

Feedback: as the statement suggests, children 'may' experience these repetitive body movement symptoms, but it cannot be concluded as the conclusion claims that children will 'definitely' experience the symptoms. Also, the conclusion only refers to body rocking, it does not refer to the other symptoms stated such as pacing or hand flapping.

INTERPRETATION – EXAMPLE 8

Statement:

Children who have autistic tendencies may suffer with repetitive body movements such as rocking, pacing or hand flapping. Many autistic children suffer relatively delayed responses and therefore this affects their development process.

Proposed Conclusion:

Children's development process can be delayed by suffering with autistic tendencies.

Conclusion Follows	Conclusion Does Not Follow
✓	

Feedback: the conclusion clearly refers back to the consequence (delayed children's development) with the initial action or cause (suffering autistic tendencies). Therefore the conclusion can be interpreted and made from the statement provided.

QUESTION 37

Statement:

Blood clots are increasing after a person undergoes surgery. A British man died after developing deep vein thrombosis (DVT), a blood clot in the leg, partly because of dehydration and travelling overseas in cramped conditions after having surgery only a few weeks before.

Proposed Conclusion:

If you suffer with dehydration, you will develop a blood clot.

Conclusion Follows	Conclusion Does Not Follow
	X

QUESTION 38

Statement:

Blood clots are increasing after a person undergoes surgery. A British man died after developing deep vein thrombosis (DVT), a blood clot in the leg, partly because of dehydration and travelling overseas in cramped conditions after having surgery only a few weeks before.

Proposed Conclusion:

There are several ways in which a blood clot can form.

Conclusion Follows	Conclusion Does Not Follow
X	

QUESTION 39

Statement:

Smoking is underlined by doctors and health experts as a cause of serious health issues. About 90% of lung cancer cases were smokers. This is due to smoking causing people to inhale a number of different toxic substances.

Proposed Conclusion:

Everyone who has lung cancer was a smoker.

Conclusion Follows	Conclusion Does Not Follow
	X

QUESTION 40

Statement:

Smoking is underlined by doctors and health experts as a cause of serious health issues. About 90% of lung cancer cases were smokers. This is due to smoking causing people to inhale a number of different toxic substances.

Proposed Conclusion:

Smokers who have lung cancer are more at risk to develop coronary heart disease.

Conclusion Follows	Conclusion Does Not Follow
	X

QUESTION 41

Statement:

Smoking is underlined by doctors and health experts as a cause of serious health issues. About 90% of lung cancer cases were smokers. This is due to smoking causing people to inhale a number of different toxic substances.

Proposed Conclusion:

Smoking can cause severe health issues including lung cancer.

Conclusion Follows	Conclusion Does Not Follow
X	

QUESTION 42

Statement:

The courts will only allow restraining orders to be permitted when sentencing or dealing with a conviction of harassment or fear of violence. This order intends to give protection for supposed victims of violence or harassment.

Proposed Conclusion:

Any one is able to get a restraining order permitted.

Conclusion Follows	Conclusion Does Not Follow
	X

QUESTION 43

Statement:

A stroke is a serious illness. A lot of awareness has been given to finding the symptoms at the earliest stage; treating a stroke is really a rush against time. Strokes occur when blood clots prevent the blood supply from reaching the brain and deprives the brain of sugar and oxygen levels. Although some research indicates that some brain cells can function without oxygen.

Proposed Conclusion:

Depriving the brain with blood and oxygen supply is the reason that people experience strokes.

Conclusion Follows	Conclusion Does Not Follow
	X

QUESTION 44

Statement:

A stroke is a serious illness. A lot of awareness has been given to finding the symptoms at the earliest stage; treating a stroke is really a rush against time. Strokes occur when blood clots prevent the blood supply from reaching the brain and deprives the brain of sugar and oxygen levels. Although some research indicates that some brain cells can function without oxygen.

Proposed Conclusion:

If people who suffer a stroke do not receive treatment quickly, they will not survive.

Conclusion Follows	Conclusion Does Not Follow
	X

QUESTION 45

Statement:

Everyone who suffers with depression also experiences some form of personal battle. For example, Chloe split from her husband while Chris lost his home.

Proposed Conclusion:

Chris lost his house because of his depression.

Conclusion Follows	Conclusion Does Not Follow
	X

QUESTION 46

Statement:

Everyone who suffers with depression also experiences some form of personal battle. For example, Chloe split from her husband while Chris lost his house.

Proposed Conclusion:

People who experience personal battles always suffer with depression.

Conclusion Follows	Conclusion Does Not Follow

QUESTION 47

Statement:

A study shows that around 25% of the British population are overweight. This is almost double what it was ten years ago. 15% of those people who are overweight are considered obese. Research has shown studies that link obesity with alcoholism and fast food.

Proposed Conclusion:

Eating fast food will make you obese.

Conclusion Follows	Conclusion Does Not Follow

QUESTION 48

Statement:

A study shows that around 25% of the British population are overweight. This is almost double what it was ten years ago. 15% of those people who are overweight are considered obese. Research has shown studies that link obesity with alcoholism and fast food.

Proposed Conclusion:

There are 25,000 more British overweight people now as opposed to ten years ago.

Conclusion Follows	Conclusion Does Not Follow

BAR COURSE APTITUDE TEST (BCAT)
TEST SECTION 5: EVALUATION OF ARGUMENTS

INSTRUCTIONS

Recognising and evaluating arguments is crucial at determining whether or not the argument works. It is important to evaluate whether an argument is strong enough to form a clear and concise dispute.

For an argument to be strong, it must show importance and directly relate to the statement or question being argued. Weak arguments tend to have missing information or leave out important elements of the question and therefore this plays no significant relevance in forming an argument.

For example, if a person were to ask someone whether they should go to university, and their response was 'you have nothing else to do'; this forms no clear logic or no real significance and therefore the argument would be classified as **weak**.

For each argument, you will be given a statement or passage to read, you will answer either:

Argument Strong – if you think the argument provides strong explanations, evidence and data, and is directly linked to the statement.

Argument Weak – if you think the argument is missing important information, misinterprets the information or does not show any direct link to the statement provided.

ARGUMENTS – EXAMPLE 9

Statement:

Should all young adults be made to take parental classes at school?

Proposed Argument:

Yes, more young adults are becoming parents, so it would be beneficial for them to learn the knowledge and skills required to look after a baby.

Argument Strong	Argument Weak
✓	

Feedback: the conclusion provides a clear and concise argument, that relates directly back to the statement. It provides the action (taking parental classes at school) and gives an example as to how it will benefit and the reason why they should (more young adults becoming parents) – therefore this is a strong and reasonable argument to make.

ARGUMENT – EXAMPLE 10

Statement:

Should all young adults be made to take parental classes at school?

Proposed Argument:

No, they are too young to be taught about parenting.

Argument Strong	Argument Weak
	✓

Feedback: although it gives a reason as to why young adults shouldn't be made to take parental classes at school, it does not expand enough on its argument's point. It is very vague and therefore limits the argument. Thus, the argument is weak.

QUESTION 49

Statement:

Should the death penalty be allowed in the UK?

Proposed Argument:

No, the death penalty does not set a good example.

Argument Strong	Argument Weak
	X

QUESTION 50

Statement:

Should the death penalty be allowed in the UK?

Proposed Argument:

No, the death penalty goes against our most basic human right – the right to life. Despite what people have done in the past, everyone should be given the chance for redemption.

Argument Strong	Argument Weak
X	

QUESTION 51

Statement:

Should the death penalty be allowed in the UK?

Proposed Argument:

Yes, the death penalty will provide a clear punishment that fits the crime which was committed. This penalty is used for the most serious offences; who consequently have given up their human rights, including the right to live.

Argument Strong	Argument Weak
✗	

QUESTION 52

Statement:

Should the Government fund the arts programmes?

Proposed Argument:

Yes, London's commercial theatre earns over half a billion pounds a year, so it makes a lot of profits.

Argument Strong	Argument Weak
	✗

QUESTION 53

Statement:

Should the Government fund the arts programmes?

Proposed Argument:

No, the arts programme shouldn't be allowed to have government funds due to no spare finances. The Government simply does not have enough money to waste on art programmes.

Argument Strong	Argument Weak
✗	

QUESTION 54

Statement:

Should the Government fund the arts programmes?

Proposed Argument:

Yes, art programmes are becoming increasingly popular and are more likely to increase profits for organisations, indicating it will boost economic wealth and help the Government expand their horizons and profits with getting involved with society.

Argument Strong	Argument Weak
X	

QUESTION 55

Statement:

Should social networking be monitored by the Government?

Proposed Argument:

No, the Government should not monitor social networking as they themselves show no interest in social media and they will not find it useful or beneficial. No one wants the Government to monitor social networking.

Argument Strong	Argument Weak
	X

QUESTION 56

Statement:

Should social networking be monitored by the Government?

Proposed Argument:

Yes, monitoring social networking will help maintain safety procedures of society by finding possible connections, motives or a lead into something they were looking for.

(but y)

Argument Strong	Argument Weak
	X

QUESTION 57

Statement:

Should convicted criminals be made to study the law when serving their sentence?

Proposed Argument:

Yes, some criminals would like the opportunity for forgiveness and to correct their mistakes; so teaching law will not only provide the rights and wrongs of the world, but also give them hope and motivation to redeem themselves and become a civilised citizen.

Argument Strong	Argument Weak
✓	

QUESTION 58

Statement:

Should convicted criminals be made to study the law when serving their sentence?

Proposed Argument:

No, teaching law to criminals would be ineffective because none of the criminals will show interest in the matter.

Argument Strong	Argument Weak
	X

QUESTION 59

Statement:

Should students be made to learn a foreign language?

Proposed Argument:

No, some students struggle with their own language, so teaching a foreign language will only confuse them more and therefore create issues around lack of confidence and motivation, which will affect their learning.

Argument Strong	Argument Weak
X	

QUESTION 60

Statement:

Should students be made to learn a foreign language?

Proposed Argument:

Yes, society is becoming more multi-cultural and a lot of jobs value employees who can speak another language, so teaching a foreign language to students will provide well rounded workers with knowledge and skills to fit in with the multi-cultural society of today.

Argument Strong	Argument Weak
X	

MOCK TEST SECTION – ANSWERS

INFERENCE

Q1.

Probably true. We can reasonably infer that the headmaster showed little concern over the situation being bullying. His reaction of emphasising the distinctions between certain kinds of behaviour could suggest he imagined more considerable circumstances.

Q2.

Insufficient data. There is no data or information to determine how many procedures are in place regarding anti-social behaviour. Therefore, it is unreasonable to claim that there is 'none'; we can assume the school has procedures in place but from the statement provided, we cannot infer this as definite.

Q3.

Insufficient data. There is no data in the statement provided to suggest that her son got hurt when the chair was pulled out from underneath him, therefore there is no evidence to back this claim up, or to disregard it.

Q4.

Probably true. This is likely to be true. Although Martin does not state the fact; his actions of having to pay a fine because he broke the no smoking regulation, suggests that this is likely to be true, but cannot be taken as definite.

Q5.

True. Martin was caught smoking in a no smoking zone three times. That means that even if each of those occasions happened once a week, that means that there is one week left in the month where Martin was not fined, therefore this inference is true.

Q6.

Insufficient data. There is no data to suggest that Martin values the privacy and rights to do what he wants more so than other people's health. Therefore this inference cannot be concluded as there is no evidence to support the claim.

Q7.

Insufficient data. There is no data to suggest that the students are Art students. You cannot conclude from the statement what the students study, so therefore there is no sufficient data.

Q8.

Probably true. Based on the statement, the routine of her son suggests that he will be the baby to cry at 5pm, therefore it is likely to be true that it will be her son who will be crying.

Q9.

False. The statement claims that the man in the balaclava pointed the gun and demanded money from 'her' till, which 'she' handed over, therefore this inference is false.

Q10.

Insufficient data. There is no evidence to indicate who or if anyone was shot. The statement does not give any information, so therefore the inference does not have sufficient data.

Q11.

Insufficient data. There is no evidence to indicate if the robber got away with the money, therefore this inference cannot be drawn from the statement provided.

Q12.

Insufficient data. There is no data provided in the statement that links gang crime with ethnic and cultural backgrounds, therefore this inference cannot be drawn.

Pass (Marginal)	45-49	Those in this category are likely to find the type of complex analysis and decision-making required on the Bar Professional Training Course challenging and may need to invest more time and effort in the course than most to meet the required standard. Available data on outcomes on the BPTC for candidates in this score range indicates that: • 0.7% have achieved a grade of 'Outstanding' • 25.4% have achieved a grade of 'Very Competent' • 26.1% have achieved a grade of 'Competent' • 47.8% have failed or not yet completed the course
Pass	50-60	Individuals scoring in this band are likely to be able to demonstrate the level of critical thinking necessary for effective analysis and decision-making on the Bar Professional Training Course. Available data on outcomes on the BPTC for candidates in this score range indicates that: • 9.4% have achieved a grade of 'Outstanding' • 55.5% have achieved a grade of 'Very Competent' • 15.6% have achieved a grade of 'Competent' • 19.5% have failed or not yet completed the course
Pass (Strong)	61-80	Individuals scoring in this band are likely to demonstrate or exceed the level of critical thinking necessary for effective analysis and decision-making on the Bar Professional Training Course. Available data on outcomes on the BPTC for candidates in this score range indicates that: • 34.4% have achieved a grade of 'Outstanding'

BAR COURSE APTITUDE TEST (BCAT) FEEDBACK REPORT

Candidate: John R Steel

ID: BCAT0009657

Score Category	Score Range	Implications
Fail	20-44	Those in this category are likely to struggle greatly with the type of complex analysis and decision-making required on the Bar Professional Training Course. In comparison with others that have completed the test, they will tend to apply faulty logic or reasoning when analysing information.

RECOGNITION OF ASSUMPTIONS

Q13.

Assumption made. This is a reasonable assumption to make. If the physician is talking to the lady about the health benefits of plums, it indicates that she has one of those health problems.

Q14.

Assumption not made. It is not clear whether eating a plum increases or decreases a person's blood pressure, therefore you are unable to jump to this assumption.

Q15.

Assumption made. It is clear from the statement provided that common courtesy and respect are signs of success. The statement indicates that lack of common courtesy and lack of respect equals to being unsuccessful, therefore this assumption can be made.

Q16.

Assumption not made. The statement does not mention anything about work ethic or motivation, so therefore the assumption cannot be drawn upon.

Q17.

Assumption made. The statement implies that employees' performance and work behaviour are factors of a successful business. Therefore employers will be expected to run a smooth and efficient workforce, thus this assumption can be made.

Q18.

Assumption not made. The statement does not mention anything about aggression or other influential factors. It only states that they are an influence in a child's life. Therefore this assumption cannot be made due to the lack of examples regarding influences.

Q19.

Assumption made. The fact that the statement claims that celebrities have an 'increasing' influential factor means that it's more of an influence now than it was in the past, therefore you can assume that celebrities play a larger part in children's lives as opposed to in the past.

Q20.

Assumption not made. The statement mentions 'certain areas' and in particular the 'South' of the UK. Therefore this assumption does not follow as it claims that 'all' of the UK should be prepared, when the statement is only talking about certain areas.

Q21.

Assumption not made. The statement does not mention anything about landscapes or protecting grass and our gardens. Therefore this assumption cannot be drawn as it does not mention these precautionary factors.

Q22.

Assumption made. The statement clearly indicates that 'if' the rainfall continues to persist, then the South of the UK will need to be ready and take action. Therefore this assumption can be made.

Q23.

Assumption not made. The statement does not mention anything about blueberries being the only way to help and control blood sugar levels, there are likely to be other alternatives. Therefore this assumption cannot be made.

Q24.

Assumption made. The statement suggests that eating blueberries helps lower blood sugar levels. This means that someone with high blood sugar levels may find eating blueberries will help lower their blood sugar levels, therefore this assumption can be drawn upon.

DEDUCTION

Q25.

Conclusion does not follow. The statement indicates ambition and motivation as important factors. This does not mean that success will come if you are ambitious and motivated; there may be several other factors that you need to consider.

Q26.

Conclusion does not follow. The statement indicates a clear link between ambition and motivation. Everyone who is ambitious are motivated, and vice versa. Therefore this conclusion does not follow.

Q27.

Conclusion does not follow. The statement mentions an employer's preference as to the type of person he wants to employ; needless to say this might not be the case for 'every' employer and therefore managerial roles might require different attributes.

Q28.

Conclusion follows. The statement mentions that health issues work alongside psychological problems. Therefore it can be concluded that every alcoholic who experiences health issues will experience psychological problems also.

Q29.

Conclusion does not follow. The statement mentions that alcoholics experience psychological problems. However, what the statement fails to mention is the types of psychological issues. Every alcoholic is likely to experience different forms of psychological problems, therefore not all of them will experience social anxiety.

Q30.

Conclusion follows. The statement claims that only people who lack leadership lack confidence, therefore people who are leaders will be confident.

Q31.

Conclusion does not follow. The statement indicates the two types of people, a leader and a follower. However, the statement does not mention anything about the traits of a follower, therefore this conclusion does not necessarily follow on from the statement.

Q32.

Conclusion does not follow. The statement mentions that children with dyslexia have some form of social anxiety. However, the statement does not mention that they struggle in school. Some children with dyslexia may prove themselves in a school environment.

Q33.

Conclusion does not follow. This statement does not follow because it does not give any indication to the progression of children who suffer with dyslexia.

Q34.

Conclusion follows. The fact the statement mentions that all children with dyslexia suffer some level of social anxiety, means that social anxiety has to be one of the symptoms of suffering with dyslexia, therefore the conclusion does follow.

Q35.

Conclusion does not follow. The statement indicates that children growing up without a father suffer 'more' psychological problems. Therefore, the conclusion does not follow in that children who do grow up with a father may still experience psychological problems.

Q36.

Conclusion follows. The statement indicates the action (children growing up without a father) and the consequence (psychological problems). Therefore, the conclusion follows by demonstrating the common issue regarding parenthood and psychological problems.

INTERPRETATION

Q37.

Conclusion does not follow. Although the statement indicates dehydration as one of the reasons the man developed deep vein thrombosis, the statement also indicates another factor. Therefore, it is impractical to come to the conclusion that if someone suffers dehydration, they will develop a blood clot, this may not be the case.

Q38.

Conclusion follows. The statement suggests three reasons as to how the man may have developed a blood clot – surgery, dehydration and cramped conditions. Therefore, it can be concluded and interpreted that blood clots can form from several possibilities.

Q39.

Conclusion does not follow. The statement clearly suggests that 90% of lung cancer cases are caused by smoking. Therefore you cannot assume that everyone who has lung cancer was a smoker, clearly at least 10% of people who developed lung cancer were non-smokers.

Q40.

Conclusion does not follow. The statement does not mention anything about coronary heart disease. It only refers to lung cancer, therefore it is impractical and illogical and cannot be concluded.

Q41.

Conclusion follows. The first sentence in the statement mentions that smoking causes serious health issues. Note the plural use of 'issues', suggesting more than one. Therefore you can conclude that smoking can cause other severe health issues including lung cancer (as stated in the statement provided).

Q42.

Conclusion does not follow. The statement indicates that only people who were sentenced or showed some form of conviction in regards to harassment or violence were given a restraining order.

Q43.

Conclusion does not follow. The statement indicates that strokes are caused by lack of blood supply which deprives the brain from receiving oxygen as well as sugar. Therefore, this conclusion is only part of the reason and thus cannot work as a conclusion for this statement.

Q44.

Conclusion does not follow. Although the statement mentions that treating a stroke is a rush against time, it does not state that it leads to a death of a person; it might suggest it kills the brain cells. Therefore you cannot conclude this from the statement provided.

Q45.

Conclusion follows. The conclusion does follow on from the statement because it states that depression leads to personal problems, which for Chris was losing his house.

Q46.

Conclusion does not follow. The conclusion cannot follow because not everyone with personal battles has depression. Although the statement links depression with suffering personal battles, it does not mean that this works the other way round.

Q47.

Conclusion does not follow. The conclusion cannot work because the statement refers to alcoholism as well as fast food, therefore fast food may not cause someone to become obese – there may be other factors (like alcoholism) to consider.

Q48.

Conclusion does not follow. You cannot come to this conclusion on the pure basis that the statement offers no data as to how many people were researched, therefore it may be more or less than this number; you simply have no evidence to work from in order for this conclusion to be true, therefore this conclusion cannot be drawn.

EVALUATION OF ARGUMENTS

Q49.

Argument weak. Although the argument is true in what it is saying, it shows no clear logic or evidence to support this claim, it does not explain the claim enough to make it a strong argument; therefore the argument is weak.

Q50.

Argument strong. The argument provides a clear claim, a reason why, and a benefit of not executing a person, therefore the argument is strong.

Q51.

Argument strong. The argument is a strong and concise debate as to why the death penalty should be allowed in the UK. It gives reason and explanation and an example to support the argument and therefore provides a logical and direct approach in relation to the statement.

Q52.

Argument weak. This argument is too generalised. There are lots of assumptions from this conclusion and that makes the argument questionable. Just because the London commercial theatre made a lot of money, it is by no accounts an overview of how well other art programmes are doing.

Q53.

Argument weak. This argument is very basic. Although the statement may be valid in that the Government do not have the right funds to fund such programmes, it does not explain it or give an example or consequence. It is just a claim, and therefore makes the argument weak.

Q54.

Argument strong. The argument provides clear explanations, reasoning and benefits of the Government funding the arts programmes, so therefore creates a strong and reasonable argument.

Q55.

Argument weak. The argument is too generalised. The claim that the Government will not find it useful or beneficial; it is not supported or reasoned and creates lots of assumptions. The fact that it states that the Government shows no interest, is also generalised, some may find it interesting and helpful.

Q56.

Argument strong. The argument provides an explanation of the reasons why the Government should monitor social networking. It links this action to possible benefits (tackling leads and motives that they are following) and thus providing a safer community.

Q57.

Argument strong. The argument provides a clear claim, a reason why, and a benefit of criminals being made to study the law.

Q58.

Argument weak. The argument is too generic. It claims that most people will not show any interest; this might not be the case. Some criminals may want to find a way for redemption and forgiveness; other criminals may have been wrongly accused, so this conclusion is too assuming to suggest no one will take any interest.

Q59.

Argument strong. The argument provides solid reasoning and examples as to why students should not be made to study a foreign language. The argument is strong because it shows clear and concise logic in relation to the statement.

Q60.

Argument strong. The argument provides a clear claim, a reason why, and a benefit of students being made to study another language.

CHAPTER 7

Scoring Criteria

Once you have completed your test, you will then be given a report with your score. You will either score a 'pass', 'marginal fail' or 'significant fail'.

Your score for the test should be considered carefully in regards to your next step in terms of your career path.

Note: As mentioned in the Introduction, we are unable to provide you with the exact number of questions you have to get right in order to pass the Bar Course Aptitude Test. This information is not available, and therefore you will want to ensure you are fully prepared and understand the requirements of the test before you set out to take it.

Although we are unable to provide you with the exact number of how many questions you should be aiming to get right in order to pass, we can provide you with the scoring criteria used to assess a candidate's abilities and critical awareness.

It goes without saying, your aim is to try and answer as many questions correctly. Do not leave out any answers; even if you do not know the answer, you are given multiple choices, so you might as well choose one and who knows; it might be the correct answer!

The next couple of pages contain the criteria that you should read in relation to the score category that you received. Read through carefully and identify your strengths and weaknesses to assess your abilities and critical thinking.

Score Category	Implications
Fail (significant)	Those who score a significant fail struggle to understand complex and critical decision making skills. Candidates show weak ability to distinguish between solid logic and reasoning with faults and misinterpretations. Candidates are likely to show: • Misconceptions to situations. • Inability to identify valid arguments or strong information. • Lack the ability to show logic or reasoning in critical analysis. • Inability to draw conclusions, and rely heavily on assumptions. • Overlook vital information that misinterprets the situation.
Fail (marginal)	Those who score a marginal fail may struggle with showing high levels of critical understanding, and are likely to struggle with decision making skills and interpretation. Candidates are likely to: • Display inabilities to interpret situations in the correct manner. • Inability to identify strong and clear arguments, and base answers on faulty reasoning and interpretation. • Draw upon conclusions with little evidence or support. • Rely on a great deal of assumptions. • Overlook important information that eliminates clear and objective interpretations.

Pass	Candidates who score in this band demonstrate high levels of critical understanding and awareness and are able to reflect clear and concise arguments. Candidates are likely to show: • A good understanding of identifying strong arguments. • The ability to recognise important information and identify clear and effective decision making skills and critical awareness. • An ability to apply solid reasoning and logic to form strong conclusions and arguments. • The ability to show critical development with rational and concise arguments that are supported, well versed and do not rely on a great deal of assumption.

CHAPTER 8

*Key Information
about the Bar Course
Aptitude Test*

OTHER KEY INFORMATION FOR THE BCAT

Here is some key information and frequently asked questions (FAQ's) about the Bar Course Aptitude Test. You should take the time to read through this section carefully in order to make yourself fully prepared for the test.

FAQ'S

- **Why do I have to take the BCAT?**

  A BCAT pass is a core requirement for anyone wanting to become a barrister and take the Bar Professional Training Course (BPTC). Without the BCAT, candidates will not be able to study the BPTC.

- **How much does it cost to take the BCAT?**

  At the time of print, the BCAT test will cost £150 for those taking it in the UK and £170 for those taking the test around the rest of the world. So you want to try and make sure that you are fully prepared and are able to pass it first time.

- **If I don't pass, can I retake the test?**

  Yes; you are able to sit the test as many times as it takes for you to pass. Be warned that each time you resit the test, you will be required to pay £150 for those in the UK and £170 for the test being taken in the rest of the world. Also, keep in mind that you have to wait 30 days in between resits.

- **If I pass the test, what happens next?**

  The BPTC Provider will be notified of your pass for the Bar Course Aptitude Test, and you will then be able to apply to take the BPTC.

- **How long are my results valid for?**

  Your BCAT results are valid for up to 5 years, after that the test will have to be retaken.

- **Do I need to notify the Bar Standards Board when I pass the BCAT?**

  No; The Bar Standards Board will be automatically notified of your pass result by Pearson Vue. Please retain your feedback report as you will be required to present this report when you take the BPTC.

- **Where can I get further information on the BCAT test and other information regarding becoming a barrister?**

  http://www.barstandardsboard.org.uk

  This website will tell you all the information about the BCAT test, FAQ's, BCAT handbook, Extenuating Circumstance forms and other important information.

Good luck with your BCAT and we wish you all the best in your future career endeavours!

The how2become team

The How2become team

Get more books, manuals, online tests and training courses at:

www.How2Become.com

23437059R00101

Printed in Great Britain
by Amazon